The Kingdom –
Here be Dragons, Here be Dreams

Joanne Rolston

Copyright

Copyright © 2015 by Joanne Rolston
All rights reserved. This book or any portion thereof may not be reproduced or used in any manner whatsoever without the express written permission of the publisher except for the use of brief quotations in a book review or scholarly journal.
First Printing: 2015

ISBN
978-0-473-33892-3

Published by JKR Publishing
36 Hutchison Cres
Wanganui
New Zealand
Kingdom777.wordpress.com

Dedication

This book is dedicated to *the King eternal, immortal, invisible, the only God, be honour and glory for ever and ever.*
1 Timothy 1:17.

The characters in this book, from whom I learned so much.
As iron sharpens iron, so one man sharpens another.
Proverbs 27:17

Especially my friends, who witnessed all of this.
A friend loves at all times, and a brother is born for adversity,
Proverbs 17:17

And my family who journeyed with me; my son Justin, daughter Nicole and husband Bert, my Isaac.

Contents

Preface 7
Prologue 3
   The hungry years..6
   The Accuser of the Brethren 9
Chapter One 12
   Salvation 18
   The Kingdom of God within..21
   The Staff..25
   The encounter in the valley 26
   The Spirit received 29
   The death...33
   The dream of my Father...36
   The place of healing..39
Chapter Two...43
   Contact 47
   The Princess 51
   The gift of the Shepherd 53
   The word at the levelled hill 56
   Coal under pressure...59
   The Riddler 61
   The Mighty Counsellor 65
   The Sword of the Spirit..68
Chapter Three...73
   The victory in the Pits 76
   The Breastplate of Righteousness 80
   The warning 84
   The promise 87
   The decision..89
   The first wish 93
   The Minstrel..95
   Kate and the crocodile 100
   Standing in the gap..105
   View from the mountain 108
Chapter Four 112
   The second wish..116

- The circle begins 119
- Dalliance 121
- The Crossroads 123
- Pearls to pigs 126
- The House of the Fathers 132
- Rebuilding the wall 134
- Liang 137

Chapter Five 138
- The winds of change 143
- The rock face 145
- Doubt, and the King's answer 147
- The Father 151
- The Father's Response 155
- When God waits 157
- Almond Grove 159
- Millennium 161

Chapter Six 164
- The small promise 166
- The Doldrums 169
- The Valley of Baca 172
- Ishmael 176
- The River 183
- His purpose 185
- The wedding ring 186
- Wellspring 189

Chapter Seven 193
- The Door of Hope, and the third wish 197
- A new thing 200
- Full circle 204
- Prince Mentor 207
- American eagle 209
- A message from the King 212
- The Well of Salvation 215
- The Deceptive Brook 218
- Sparks and sparring 221

Chapter Eight 223
- Choosing the Chosen 228
- Issac 235

The courtship	238
Isaac proposes	241
Shelter in the storm	243
Turning north	245
Mahurangi, Open Heaven	250
Treasures of darkness	254
The seed	260
The Year of Inheritance	264
Epilogue	271
Shepherds Call	274
An invitation	276
Glossary	278
The Author	280

Preface

In New Zealand we use the expression "I've lost the plot." This is a story about how I *found* the plot; a plot which developed slowly while reading the Bible and writing a rough journal about my spiritual journey with God. I came to realise the plot started before I was even born.

The plot is about a family, a lost inheritance, and the many trials we must go through to enter the Kingdom of God.

The story starts with Anna, my great-great grandmother. Her words helped guide me back to the Father.

This is one of the things she wrote; *"Trust the Lord in your ways and free yourself of your troubles. Trust His fatherly care, before him nothing is too hard or too large that He cannot guide and lead you by the glory of His name to greater love and happiness. Of all the people and possessions, my saviour is still nearest to me. The Lord sees into your heart."* Anna Dassler 1932

It took me a long time to realise that an ancestor's legacy of faith was God's gift to me.

The Lord thinks generationally whereas we tend to think everything revolves around 'me.' The Lord is thinking of the 'big picture' while we often can't see beyond our small world.
He is looking ahead to the generations to come and saying, "There is more at stake here."

The big picture is like a beautiful garment. We spin the yarn, but it gets tangled and there's way too much scarlet in it. The thread is untangled, exchanged for gold, and woven into a pattern in the fabric of redemption. I think the thread was exchanged by the King at his arrest and trial. Mocked by the Roman soldiers, Jesus wore the scarlet robe for us.

Psalm 45 inspired me to seek the Kingdom of God. It's a

wedding song which speaks of a princess wearing a gown interwoven with gold;

All glorious is the princess within her chamber; her gown is interwoven with gold.
In embroidered garments she is led to the king; her virgin companions follow her — those brought to be with her. Led in with joy and gladness, they enter the palace of the king. Psalm 45:13-15.

You'll see the scarlet thread in the story, and you'll see where it has been interwoven with the gold. Scripture references are mainly from the NIV unless marked otherwise.

My inspiration is the King. To him belongs the Kingdom, the power, and the glory.

"You are a king, then!" said Pilate. Jesus answered, "You are right in saying I am a king. In fact, for this reason I was born, and for this I came into the world, to testify to the truth. Everyone on the side of truth listens to me."

Prologue

Newly arrived from Hamburg, the sailing ship slowly approached the long shingle spit that connected the town of Napier with the harbour. The groaning of its timbers and the creaking of its rigging as it ploughed its way across the ocean had now ceased. Sails furled, the German flag flying at the stern bespoke her country. It was August 1875 - winter in the southern hemisphere.

The immigrants mounted the bulwark, anxiously awaiting the arrival of the health and immigration officers. The new arrivals presented a somewhat novel spectacle from the nations there represented — Germans, Danes, Swedes, Norwegians and Poles, all chattering in the language and dialects of their respective countries. They all expressed concern that they couldn't speak English.

For a brief period of three years in the 1870's, the New Zealand government opened the door for Northern Europeans. The door soon closed after they realised it was more difficult to settle immigrants who didn't speak the language.

Anna Dassler, a German immigrant, stood on the bulwark with her husband Wilhelm, holding her baby son.

The next day the passengers were put ashore in lighters and landed at the Spit – a thin gravel beach fronting a shallow inland harbour. The cargo was unpacked from the ship's holds and carters shouting in English put their trunks on wagons. They walked up Barrack Hill to the immigration barracks, their home for the next three weeks.

As they settled into the immigration barracks Anna strained to hear Wilhelm against the clamour in the dormitory. It was getting frustratingly hard for her to hear anything after a voyage in which she'd endured sea sickness and ear infections. In two years, she would go completely deaf and be unable to learn English.

Seeking solitude after the cramped quarters of the ship and dormitory, Anna surveyed the new land from her vantage point on Barrack Hill.

The town of Napier with its newly constructed timber buildings occupied a narrow strip of land at the bottom of the hill, between the beach and the inland harbour. To the east she could see another vessel on the horizon, sailing into port from the Pacific Ocean.

Her eyes traced the road along the beach they would soon follow by bullock wagon. The road merged with the shingle beach, turning into a rough track that disappeared south-west. The country looked wild and untamed; nothing like Berlin with its paved streets, squares, cathedrals and grand buildings. Ranges dusted with snow capped the horizon.

A Monarch butterfly, another recent arrival to New Zealand, alighted on a Kotukutuku shrub near her, seeking nectar from the pink and purple flowers.

Anna looked to her God. He seemed as unfathomable as this new country.
"Father, we're now at the ends of the earth. Guide us, for we are pilgrims and strangers here."

Quietly she prayed the words from Psalm 61 (NIV); *"Hear my cry, O God; Listen to my prayer. From the ends of the earth I call to you, I call as my heart grows faint; Lead me to the rock that is higher than I."*

Anna did not have any difficulty hearing the Lord. He spoke in her voice and language but with his own measured words, saying; *"For I the Lord am bringing you into a good land—a land with brooks, streams, and deep springs gushing out into the valleys and hills; a land with wheat and barley, vines, fig trees and honey; a land where bread will not be scarce and you will lack nothing." Deuteronomy 8:7-9 (NIV)*

Young and full of hope, Anna looked forward to the life they would build at the ends of the earth. Coming from a well-to-do family, she'd been fortunate. Her father was a Wachtmeister - a mounted policeman in Prussia, northern Germany. She'd been privately educated and they'd lacked nothing, until her father's dishonest lawyer absconded with the family's money.

Unbelievably, their local Catholic priest allied himself with the crooked lawyer; and so her father withdrew the family from the church. The priest then excommunicated the whole family, including the descendants.

The Lord could see that Anna was still worried about their banishment from the church by the priest. "No man can shut the door but me," he reassured her. "I've given my servants, my called-out ones, the keys to the Kingdom.

You don't need a priest to unlock the door. *Ask and it will be given to you; seek and you will find; knock and the door will be opened to you,*" he promised, speaking from Matthew 7:7 (NIV).

Reassured, Anna smiled. This was a new start. The Lord had opened a door to this young country at the ends of the earth, and their children would be born of a different nation. "Will your blessing be upon the children born here?" she asked.

"I promise you the blessing of an open heaven, but it will depend on the family keeping faith with me," he replied, adding; *"How gladly would I treat you like my children and give you a pleasant land, the most beautiful inheritance of any nation, if I thought you would call me 'Father' and not turn away from following me." Isaiah 61:4 (NIV)*

The hungry years

Four years after their arrival in New Zealand a depression gripped the land, leading into years they called "the hungry eighties." In the year 1886, Wilhelm sat at the bank manager's desk nervously holding his hat while the bank manager examined his farm accounts.

He was being pressured to sell their wool for a pittance, but debt was a trap he did not want to get into. He'd worked too hard and come too far to be pushed into indentured servitude.

Fixing his eyes on the bank manager, he said "No, I will not sell my wool for that price. I will wait until the wool prices are better."
A large wooden clock ticked slowly on the wall while Wilhelm calmly waited for his response. He waited, staring out the window at the main street of Waipawa.

They'd lived in the wilderness to start with, after being allotted a fifty-acre section in heavy bush with no road access, in a remote area called 'Makaretu'. Wilhelm was unhappy about going to Makaretu, but he had no choice. Friberg, the man in charge of the immigrants did not like him. He had too much education for Friberg's liking.

Times were hard and there was nothing to be made off the land at first. Wilhelm had just five pounds in his pocket when they landed at Napier, and his first job was at a market garden in the nearby town of Hastings, digging potatoes for the Maoris at six shillings per day.

Working for them meant he had to be away for up to a week at a time. He'd often carry a large sack of potatoes home, hoisted onto his back by two Maoris. He dared not put it down to rest as he would not have been able to pick it up again.

Anna stayed at Takapau while Wilhelm built a rough dwelling of Totara slabs with a shingle roof from the trees he cleared from the site. A fireplace of slabs lined with packed clay completed the crude dwelling.

Eventually they carved a farm out of the bush and built a four roomed house. Wilhelm established a flock of around 200 sheep. Then the depression hit.

And now he'd travelled to the bank at Waipawa, where he was trying to negotiate terms for credit.

"If you will not sell your wool, we cannot offer you any credit," the bank manager told him.

"Very well, we will live without writing any cheques," Wilhelm declared in his heavily accented English, picking up his hat. "Good luck and good day to you" the bank manager responded curtly.

"The Lord will provide," Anna replied when Wilhelm told her the bad news.

Three years later Wilhelm rode back to the town of Waipawa, debt free, to triumphantly show the bank manager his wool cheque.
Ten years later, in 1898, Wilhelm died of stomach cancer.

Anna was left in deep mourning with eight children, seven sons and a daughter. Half of them were under the age of twelve. Albert, her youngest, was only six.

Utterly bereft, she wept; "Father, when you called us to go to this place we would later receive as our inheritance, we obeyed and went, even though we did not know where we were going. By faith we made our home in the land you promised, like a stranger in a foreign country. We lived in tents, as did Isaac and Jacob, children who were heirs of the same promise. But now I am a widow, a stranger in a strange land. Where is the blessing you promised?"

"I know you did not receive the things promised," the Lord comforted her. "You only saw them and welcomed them from a distance, admitting that you are a foreigner and stranger here. The inheritance will be handed on to a future generation. I have planned something better for you, so that only together with them will you be made perfect."

"Let it be so," Anna replied sorrowfully, "I will look forward to your Kingdom, of which you are the architect and builder; may your Kingdom come."

The Accuser of the Brethren

Walter, the third of Anna's seven sons, was 22 when his father died. It made sense to him to join the Oddfellows lodge, which he regarded as a friendly society. Members paid a regular subscription and in return received financial support in times of illness, and funeral funds in the event of death. He'd seen the help the lodge provided. What he had not seen was the doorway into the occult.

God the Father watched in sorrow as Walter turned away from him, ignoring his command not to follow other gods and serve them.

Blindfolded, Walter was led into the lodge meeting room. All was intense silence; broken by the howling of members and the rattling of ponderous chains. Startled, he heard a question as the noise subsided.

"What do you most want?" he was asked, in accordance with the lodge initiation.

"Light" he answered.

Lucifer laughed. He smirked; happy he'd thwarted God's purposes. He hated the children of Adam. He'd hated them ever since creation.

Family by family he fought God for them, wanting people to worship him instead. His aim was to expose people to God's wrath. All he had to do was get them to sin and run after other gods.

It had been an easy matter to tempt Anna's son into the lodge after his father Wilhelm's early death.

The devil brought his accusation before the throne of God, "Your servant's son has sworn a Freemasonry oath to me. If they bow down to me or worship me, it is written that you will punish the children for the sin of the parents to the third and fourth generation. You are a jealous God. Now I will hear your judgement over them, in accordance with the law."

He knew the consequences of idol worship written in the book of Deuteronomy.

God looked at Walter in sorrow. Forced to pronounce judgment on the family line, he said "*I the Lord will afflict you with tumours from which you cannot be cured, madness, blindness and confusion of mind. At midday you will grope about like a blind person in the dark. You will be unsuccessful in everything you do; and day after day you will be oppressed and robbed, with no one to rescue you.*" (Deuteronomy 28:27-29)

Lucifer was satisfied.

"Do not forget to add that I will show my love to a thousand generations of those who love me and keep my commandments," God reminded Lucifer, as he spoke from the same law.

"But will the generations under judgement love *you*?" Lucifer derided God.
The Lord's eyes flashed, "You will not accuse forever."
Life went on.

Walter and his two older brothers, Wilhelm and Richard, sent Anna and the five younger children to a German community in Queensland in the hope she might marry Ferdi, her widowed brother-in-law.

Lucifer continued his attack on the family through Ferdi, who was possessed of a religious spirit. Ferdi beat the children, forcing them to get up early for family prayers. Even a yawn brought punishment.

After her youngest son Albert bit Ferdi on the thigh while being spanked, Anna had enough and sailed back to New Zealand with her brood. This experience left the children with a strong dislike for religion, even though they could quote large passages of the Bible word for word.

Anna kept the faith. At the end of her life she wrote, *"Even though I have been through many rough passages; of all the people and possessions, my Saviour is still nearest to me."*

Looking to the children to receive the things God had promised, she prayed, *"I keep asking that the God of our Lord Jesus Christ, the glorious Father, may give you the Spirit of wisdom and revelation, so that you may know him better."* Ephesians 1:17 (NIV)
In the battleground for the souls of the children, her prayer came before the throne of God like incense. "How can I forget them?" God asked himself. He would look to a future generation to inherit the promises.
"I will respond to the prayer of the destitute; I will not despise their plea. Let this be written for a future generation, that a people not yet created may praise the Lord." (Psalm 102:17-18)

Anna died in 1942, and the generations continued. Joanna, a great-great grand-daughter arrived in the land at the same place that Anna had arrived. This is her story.

Chapter One

It was 1971. A slight breeze parted Joanna's short hair as she sat perched on a rock overlooking her farm, not far from Barrack Hill as the crow flies. Barrack Hill was now called Hospital Hill. Napier Hospital had been built on the site of the former Napier immigration barracks, where her ancestors had stayed on their arrival. But at age eleven Joanna knew nothing of that, or of Anna.

She looked out over the farm. The paddocks were empty, except for her horse. The cows had gone, and so had her grandparents. They'd retired in the far north, to be near the rest of the family after selling their share of the farm. She missed them so much it hurt. But she wasn't allowed to show it.

The legalistic voice of her father's oldest sister still rang in her ears; "You're not to cry, you've had them all to yourself, and now it's your cousins' turn."

Shut down, Joanna stared at the ground so the tears couldn't escape. Somehow, she said goodbye without crying. Her aunt was pleased.

Unbidden, the tears came flooding out in the classroom the day the dairy herd was sold. The teacher tried in vain to comfort her.

In her mind's eye, Joanna could still see her blind grandfather slowly walk across the fields with his walking stick to bring the cows for milking, accompanied by Tip, his three-legged dog. It was a picture of disability.

In spite of this, the cows still got milked and in time honoured fashion, Tip chased the milk tanker.

Her grandfather's name was Arch. Arch was the son of Walter, the son of Anna. Arch had followed his father into the lodge. Blind since his late twenties, he lost his sight after a cork from a ginger beer bottle hit him in the eye, and the other eye got infected. But he had the same indomitable will as Wilhelm, his grandfather. He didn't give up. He carried on farming.

In middle age he moved from his isolated farm in the foothills of the Ruahine Mountain ranges to the dairy farm near Napier when the children were ready for secondary school.

Joanna looked out to the horizon. The land had changed, but not all of it by the hand of man. The inland harbour had gone after rising two metres out of the sea in the violent shaking of the Napier earthquake, forty years before. The seabed was now farmland, and the islands had become hills.

Spread out before Joanna, the land was no longer wild and untamed as it had been in Anna's day. Farms, orchards, vineyards and small towns dotted the plain from the coast to the hills.

Joanna's eyes drank in the familiar landscape. To the south the peninsula of Cape Kidnappers jutted into the Pacific Ocean. A craggy hill named 'Te Mata Peak' reared up on the horizon to the west. A distinctive hill called the "Sugarloaf" and the Mission Monastery with its vineyards were just up the road, and the farm where Joanna lived lay below at the foot of Wharerangi Hill. Wharerangi meant the 'house of the sky or of heaven.'
If the land was in the house of heaven the door remained closed.

But it didn't matter. They'd soon be leaving Napier. Her father had decided to sell up as well. Tired of getting up at four o'clock in the morning to milk cows, he'd bought a mixed sheep and cattle farm 250 kilometres away on the west coast of the North Island, near Wanganui. She'd climbed the hill one last time to remember Napier and commit the land to memory.

Her eyes travelled to Waratai, the home she'd grown up in, three paddocks away. Waratai was a big character home with large ceilings and a long passageway, surrounded by gum and pepper trees. Behind the house there was an old cowshed where her father restored his vintage cars, and historic stables where they stored their hay.
Taipo creek flowed quietly behind the out buildings.
It was her Grandparent's cottage that she'd miss the most – not Waratai. They all had to compete for attention in their father's house. Home for her meant a place with no love.

Six children had been born in six years, when two sets of twin girls followed the birth of her brother. The eldest, she'd been lost in the crowd after the birth of the twins - especially the last set, when a nightmare mix of post-natal depression and bipolar disorder engulfed the family.

The youngest twin, a little brown-haired toddler called Luka, could not compete and rocked herself on her bed like an orphan. A typical day would begin with sounds of distress. Someone was always crying. Their irritable mother harassed them like a dog worrying sheep.

They were hit, pulled, pushed, slapped, yelled at and verbally abused. As the eldest Joanna bore the brunt of it and felt miserable.

She could not deal with her mother's highs and lows, which happened regularly and lasted for weeks. It was a recurring nightmare she could not escape from.

Her mother was a scary figure at the height of her mood swings. She'd become a tornado of activity, tearing around the countryside on mad impulses and errands, visiting relatives and friends with half dressed, grubby children. Coming down from her high, she'd be angry and agitated.

Like a tight spring, her mother would get more and more wound up and go faster and faster until *'boing'*, the spring broke.

After that she'd crash and spend days in bed, too lethargic to look after anything. When the lows came her mother could barely function or run the house – but at least the children all got some peace. The haranguing, slaps, and abuse would stop for a little while.

Chaos reigned and the house was a mess. Smelly food scraps lay in buckets and mountains of washing mouldered in the wash house. Her father rejected his damaged wife and big family, withdrawing from them. When he came in from the milking shed, there would be yelling on top of the crying.

At the breakfast table Joanna would either yell back or eat her cereal quickly so she could escape. After breakfast she would pull on dirty clothes, get her two sandwiches, and walk to the bus stop to go to school.

After school she took the billy across the paddocks to get the milk from the cowshed near her grandparent's cottage. Then she'd spend time with her Gran while her grandfather and father worked in the milking shed.

The cottage with its courtyard, trellis fence and flower filled garden was her only safe place. It was orderly, peaceful and warm, and she stayed for as long as she could.

All Joanna wanted was order, structure and boundaries, but she wasn't being given any. It came out in her behaviour. She played alone with her farm of plastic animals, putting walls and fences around everything she could. The toy farm was kept at her Grandparents. She wanted her pretend world to be safe.

Her grandparents did not know what Joanna's home life was like at their son's house. She was too ashamed to speak of it. No-one spoke about the elephant in the room.

Although Joanna did not understand, she knew something was terribly wrong. She became the family scapegoat - the target of her parent's hostility and spite.

Confused, she lost all confidence in herself, believing she must have been 'bad.' She was slapped so much during one of her mother's manic periods that she withdrew into herself and stopped talking.

Traumatised and in a world of hurt, she was given a hearing test at school because the teachers thought she'd gone deaf.

The hair colour in Joanna's family was evenly divided between blondes and brunettes. Joanna's mother preferred the blondes.

In her eighth year her unpredictable mother took a dislike to her brown hair, shaming her by getting it hacked off at the ears.

"Why can't I have long hair like my sisters?" Joanna wailed, bewildered.

She badly wanted what she was being denied - plaits, tights and nice dresses like the other girls wore at school.

"Your face is too long," her mother snapped. Annoyed at her child's distress she slapped her face hard. Cowed into silence, she was unable to understand her mother's malice and spite.

Until she was about four, Joanna had been cared for and dressed nicely. Now the shoulder length hair was gone, as were the beautiful clothes. Secretly she hungered for beautiful dresses and dance lessons. She kept dolls in her room and a small picture of ballerinas on her wall.

One day she got home from school to find the picture wasn't there. Her mother had given it away to another girl at her school.

"Why?" Joanna asked, bewildered and upset.

"Debbie does ballet and you don't," her mother snapped in a tone that brooked no argument.

No longer seeing herself as pretty, Joanna gave up. She became a 'tomboy', spending the rest of her childhood outdoors, pretending that's what she'd chosen to be. She felt out of place and was often mistaken for a boy. When that happened, she did not bother to correct the mistake. It was better to be a handsome boy rather than an ugly girl. Boys got more respect, and she got to do adventurous things. Her father said all women were crazy.

She believed him and feared growing up, afraid of being like her mother. Having no-one to model herself on, she didn't understand social cues or how to act around other people. Anxious and filled with self-loathing, she lacked confidence.

"What do you look like?" her blind grandfather once asked. Robbed of her femininity, Joanna turned away, ashamed.

Joanna realised how far she'd sunk on the social ladder at school when it came time for dancing, and the boys had to choose dance partners. No one picked her. Left standing alone red faced with shame and embarrassment; she added dancing to the list of things to fear.

The ugly short haircuts lasted until she was nearly fourteen, when she'd grown old enough to stand up to her mother.

The Lord watched Joanna, just as he'd watched Anna. She came to him in belief the year before, at the age of ten, a wounded soul seeking salvation. The idea that he could be called 'Father' never entered her head.
He longed to restore her soul. It was time for her to move. He was going to bring Joanna into greener pastures.

Salvation

Jesus said again, "Very truly I tell you, I am the gate for the sheep." John 10:7

Joanna came through 'The Gate' in 1970 at the age of ten, without realising what it was, where she was, or what had happened. All she knew was she was at her aunt's place, and unlike the other women in Joanna's life, this aunt had time for her. There was a plaque on the dining room wall of her aunt's simple little cottage that said, "Christ is the Head of this house, the Unseen Guest at every meal, the Silent Listener to every conversation."

At bedtime, her aunt had been reading to them from a series of Bible stories. Joanna was drawn to the picture on the inside cover, of Jesus wearing a white robe standing in a green field. He looked so kind. There were a lot of children gathered around him, but they were all 'good' and she was bad.

She must be bad, otherwise why was she being hit by her parents all the time? Her parents said that only good children went to Heaven. If that was true, where was she going?
She wanted to know Jesus, but did not know how to find him.

As a baby she'd been dedicated to the Lord as was the custom, and then he was forgotten. All she knew about Jesus was he lived in Heaven. Sometimes she'd sing a song to him with a wish in her heart. If she did try to come to him, would he make her go away?

The books opened the gate as she studied the picture of him. Visualising the green field and the tree he was sitting under, she erased the 'good' children from the scene so it was just her and Jesus.

"Only good children go to Heaven," the little girl heard, hindered from coming any closer. Uncertain, she stood there battling her thoughts. Unseen, a battle was being fought in the spiritual world by the angels who are appointed to serve those who will inherit salvation.

"Forbid her not to come to me; for of such is the Kingdom of Heaven" the Lord roared at the enemy.
As she approached the throne of God, the Lord's eyes softened, as he turned from the Lion into the Lamb. The child approached the Lord with longing; fearful she would be rejected.

"Jesus, I believe in you," she said, shyly touching his sleeve. "Please, I know I'm not good enough, but I want to go to Heaven when I die," she pleaded.

The Lord bent low to receive her, showing his joy in the presence of the angels, as he did each time a sinner repented. Those who wanted to enter the Kingdom had to come in faith like this child.

His joy was tinged with grief. The child had come to him as a beggar, as so many of the children of Adam did. They came to him alone, uncertain and dispossessed; like orphaned princes and princesses clad in filthy rags, not knowing who they really were. Still, they came.

If only they could *see*, if only they could *know* who they were born to be. The greatest in his kingdom were those who were like little children.
"Blessed are you who are poor in spirit, for the kingdom of heaven is yours," he promised.

This child was clad in green checked shorty pyjamas embroidered with the motif, "My heart belongs to Daddy." He smiled. Later in life he would show her the significance of those words; later in life she would know him as 'Abba.'

God the Father looked at the child with compassion. Although children came to him readily, those with unbelieving parents got left in the wilderness. He'd left instructions in Proverbs 22:6 for people to follow; *Train up a child in the way he should go: and when he is old, he will not depart from it.*

Children needed to be shown the way to him. Alone and unguided, this child would eat the bread of adversity mixed with tears.

Unheard by Joanna, Jesus said "Child, I am the Gate. You have entered by me, and you are saved."
Thinking of the valley he would move her to in a couple of years, he added *"You will go in and out and find pasture." (John 10:7)*

The Kingdom of God within

Rocking back and forwards on the wooden chair, Joanna absorbed the fire's warmth and twirled her pencil. She was still adapting to her new life in the hill country near Wanganui. They'd moved in the first week of August, 1971, just as the lambs started coming.

The primary school was a lot smaller than she was accustomed. The two-roomed country school was located at the start of the tar sealed section of road leading to town. It had been there for a century. Joanna's classroom housed the eight- to thirteen-year-olds, including her younger brother and sisters.

"Write a story about moving," the teacher asked, after discovering Joanna's talent for writing. Joanna went back to her desk, thinking about it.

The move from Hawkes Bay had been a mad escapade that ended up in the vintage car magazine under the title "How not to shift." She'd have to leave a lot of things out - like how long it took to get her horse in the float, the swearing, and all the breakdowns.

Being a typical New Zealander and a great believer in 'Do-It-Yourself,' Joanna's father did not hire a carrier for their move. Four vehicles of varying ages and states of repair left Napier in a mixed convoy. Her father's old pre-war Bedford truck led the way, towing a trailer. It had nailed on corrugated iron sides and a tarpaulin top. The corrugated iron sides leaned outwards.

Next was a Vauxhall Vanguard, towing an oversized, overweight trailer - followed by a Mark 7 Jag towing the horse-float.

Puttering along behind was her father's pride and joy, a vintage 1920 Arrol Johnson that he'd restored himself.

A disbelieving traffic cop gave her father's crazy cavalcade a very suspicious look. Not wanting the headache and mountain of paperwork he waved them on.

The first incident happened after 120 kilometres when her father drove the Bedford truck under the awning of a petrol station at Dannevirke, and got it firmly stuck. Attempting to salvage the situation he backed out, shredding the awning and tearing out the gas station lights.

Just before the Manawatu Gorge there was a terrible noise as the Jag ran over a piece of steel. They saw another piece of steel on the road just after the Gorge.

They followed the trail of steel for thirty or so kilometres, until the cavalcade ground to a halt. The Bedford's trailer had broken a spring and was now listing badly.

Soon after that the listing trailer sheared its tow ball and was only connected by the safety chain. The Vauxhall and Jag went on ahead while the vintage car puttered off to Feilding, a nearby town, to get a new tow ball.

Darkness fell and the vintage car lost its headlights. The driver, her father's best friend, blindly followed the Bedford and trailer in the pouring rain, guided only by the light reflecting off the wet road and the occasional tail light when the listing trailer went around a bend.

After delivering the horse and furniture to the new farm, the Bedford and Jag did the return trip. On the way back it was the Bedford's turn to play up. Its generator went out in sympathy with the Arrol's.

Predictably, the Bedford's battery went flat on the return trip. Five tired adults and six children detoured to the nearest town of Palmerston North to get it charged while they ate a very late meal at 11:30pm.

After installing the charged truck battery in the pouring rain, they got underway, hoping for no further incidents. But just after the Manawatu Gorge, midway between Wanganui and Hawkes Bay, the Bedford conked out again.

The Jag heroically towed the empty horse trailer *and* untrustworthy Bedford until its old engine coughed back into life. Beyond tired, they got home in the pre-dawn, at a time best described as 'stupid hour.'

Handing the story to the teacher, Joanna hoped it did not make them sound like the Beverly Hill-billies.

Later in the morning the Anglican minister came to give them religious instruction. He said something that she did not understand; "The Kingdom of God is within you."

Some Pharisees asked Jesus when the Kingdom of God would come. His answer was, "The Kingdom of God does not come in such a way as to be seen. No one will say, 'Look, here it is!' or 'There it is!' because the Kingdom of God is within you." Luke 17:20-21 (GNT)

Joanna thought about it as the school-house fire roared in the wood stove. Her brow furrowed. Here was another mad idea. How could a Kingdom be within a person?

The Lord saw her puzzlement, knowing it was too much for a child to understand. He would reveal the Kingdom when she was ready. She'd need faith to find it.

Faith came from hearing and hearing came from the *Word*. The Lord *was* the Word, and he was known as the Author and Finisher of Faith.

Turning the pages of his book, a book that was alive and active,

he looked at what he'd written; *"The Kingdom of Heaven is like treasure hidden in a field. When a man found it, he hid it again, and then in his joy went and sold all he had and bought that field."* Matthew 13:44 (NIV)
He would leave her with a treasure - the Maori word for it was 'taonga.' A taonga could be anything from a word to a memory. Would the child find the taonga, the treasure hidden in the field?

Needing a place where she could start from; something she was already familiar with and would recognise later in life, he chose the pasture in the verses of Psalm 23. He would reveal himself as the Shepherd.

The Staff

Splattered with mud, Joanna threw herself at the ewes and lambs that were dodging past her. The sheep were launching themselves into the air in every direction, with six inexperienced children trying to hold them. There were no dogs for that first muster - the children were the dogs and their father, more used to cows than sheep, shouted at them in frustration.

She tried to stop one charging ewe, only to stab her hand on a thorny stick of gorse hidden in the ewe's fleece. Another jumping ewe hit her in the chest, ran her over and kept on going.

This was the family's first muster. It was late August - the end of winter and the first month of their new lives on the sheep farm. Their arrival coincided with the lambing and docking season, one of the busiest times on the farming calendar.

They didn't know what they were doing and lacked the experience to see that the docking pen was in an impossible place.

It was stuck right in the middle of the long boundary fence they shared with Mount Zion, the sheep station in the next valley. Joanna didn't know what the previous owners were thinking; it was a stupid place to put the pen as there were no corners to herd the sheep into.

That first dock took all day. Wearily trudging home in the dark, Joanna decided to ask for a crook for her thirteenth birthday; a staff with a curved end. She hoped it would make life easier when it came to mustering sheep.

The encounter in the valley

Holding her staff, Joanna rested while she waited at the gate, helping her father move sheep. She was standing in her favourite place on the farm, a pasture called Swamp.

Swamp was situated near the woolshed and a farm cottage they called 'the Whare'. Some Maori words had found their way into their language. The word whare, pronounced 'forry', was Maori for house.

The farm lay in a lovely valley near Wanganui. The land was described as 'hard hill country' - a land of rugged slopes crowned with flat topped hills.

A narrow gravel road led to the farm and few bothered to travel it unless they had good reason. It also led to the farm near the end of the road called 'Mount Zion'. In the Kingdom, Zion is the King's holy mountain and the place where God dwells with man.

The Swamp paddock was bordered by the creek and the road. Poplars lined the road from fence battens the early settlers had used - posts which had sprouted from dry sticks into tall trees.

A proliferation of kapok, willow and elm trees grew by the bridge. Joanna found refuge in the green willows where the creek ran into a silent, sun dappled pool. It was very cool, even in summer.

The only sound was the quiet rush of the creek as it flowed over a small waterfall. The soft shadows and the rustle of trees made it a quiet, soothing place.

Pukekos with their royal blue plumage and bright orange beaks made their nests in the rushes. They called these native birds 'swamp chickens.'

Standing idle in the sun, Joanna was caught halfway between awareness and a doze. The Lord chose that moment to approach her, as she leaned on her crook, lulled by the chirping of the birds and the gurgle of the creek.

Looking at the child, he spoke the words from Psalm 23 directly into her spirit; *"I am your Shepherd. You shall not want. I have made you to rest, in this green pasture ..."*

Not hearing him, Joanna stirred, lifting her chin from its resting place on the top of her crook. She looked around, sensing him. He seemed to belong to this green pasture, or did the pasture belong to him? Her mind filled with pleasant thoughts.
The Lord continued with a promise; *"I will lead you, these quiet waters by. I will restore your soul. You will walk on the path of righteousness; even for my own name's sake."*

Satisfied with the beauty of the place he had chosen, he said; *"I will pour out my spirit on you. You will spring up like grass in this meadow, like the poplar trees by this flowing stream."* (Isaiah 44:3-4)

The Shepherd knew she could not hear his voice. He normally spoke from his word, but Joanna didn't have any Bible verses. Instead, he flooded her mind with tenderness, carefully wrapping each word as a gift.

Afterwards Joanna recalled the words as having a feeling attached to them. He talked about growing up and how great women were. His was a different voice from the biting voice of her father, who belittled women. Her father's bitterness and disapproval made her wish she had been born a boy, or not been born at all. This voice reassured her and made her feel good about growing into a woman.

It was almost like having a talk with a loving mother, except that this was a *'He.'* As he poured words of affirmation, comfort and reassurance into her inner being, Joanna felt the words warm her heart.

The sound of bleating sheep and barking dogs broke into her reverie. "Don't go," she pleaded as she felt his loving presence slowly fade.

Joanna did not tell her parents about the encounter; afraid they would scoff at her and her 'big imagination' – but she did tell her younger brother and sisters. They didn't know who 'He' was either, although Christen, one of her sisters, would have a similar encounter herself.

"Perhaps it was Mother Mary" one of her sisters suggested. They weren't Catholic, but the Beatles song "Let It Be" by the Beatles was popular at that time.

"No, it wasn't a woman. He just spoke like I imagine a loving mother would …" Joanna replied wistfully.

The Spirit received

In 1973 Joanna started secondary school at a girl's college in town. It was hard at first because she didn't know anyone, and the girls were nasty to her. At thirteen she had no idea about looks and was still being forced to wear the ugly short haircuts – except now it looked even worse because her hair was really oily.

She was looked down on. "No one wants to hear what you have to say" she was told. Bewildered, she learned they all hated her, but she didn't know what she'd done.

Surrounded by bullies, Joanna grew silent, which led to problems later on in life when she had to attend meetings at work. Eventually she found her feet and made some friends.

In 1976, her last year of school Joanna's best friend Nerida got religion. Joanna was interested in the Pentecostal church Nerida attended. She felt herself drawn to the Lord at the service, attracted by the warmth of his presence. He seemed familiar.

"Why are you all praying in different languages?" Joanna asked her friend Nerida's pastor, puzzled by their strange behaviour. She wondered how they were able to do that.
"It's in the Bible. Read the second chapter of Acts. We are only doing what they did," the pastor replied.

Joanna read about the day of Pentecost where Jesus sent his followers the Holy Spirit;
"When the day of Pentecost came, all the believers were gathered together in one place. Suddenly there was a noise from the sky which sounded like a strong wind blowing, and it filled the whole house where they were sitting.
Then they saw what looked like tongues of fire which spread out and touched each person there. They were all filled with the Holy Spirit and began to talk in other languages, as the Spirit enabled them to speak."

Acts 2:1-4 (GNT)

The apostle Peter told the crowd that gathered that the followers weren't drunk. No, this is what was spoken by the prophet Joel:

"In the last days, God says, I will pour out my Spirit on all people. Your sons and daughters will prophesy, your young men will see visions, your old men will dream dreams.
Even on my servants, both men and women, I will pour out my Spirit in those days, and they will prophesy."

Acts 2:17-18 (NIV)

She learned that the Holy Spirit was the helper Jesus spoke of when he said;
"If you love me, you will obey my commandments. I will ask the Father, and he will give you another helper, who will stay with you forever. He is the Spirit, who reveals the truth about God. The world cannot receive him, because it cannot see him or know him. But you know him, because he remains with you and is in you."
John 14:15 (GNT)

The Holy Spirit must have been the one she'd met in the pasture. This time, she wanted him to stay with her. Believing what had been written, Joanna hesitantly approached the Lord saying; "I believe in you. Will you give me the Holy Spirit?"

"You are not good enough," an accusing voice said in her mind. She faltered for a minute, but the Lord willed her to hear him instead of condemnation.

Silencing the accuser, he urged her closer, saying *"Ask, and you will receive; seek, and you will find; knock, and the door will be opened to you.*
Would a father give his son a snake when he asks for fish? Or would he give him a scorpion when he asks for an egg? As bad as people are, they know how to give good things to their children. How much more then, will the Father in heaven give the Holy Spirit to those who ask him!" (Luke 11:9-13)

Joanna was nearly knocked off her feet by the power of overwhelming love, as she received the Holy Spirit. If she wanted proof that God was real she had it, as she could now speak to him in a language she'd never learned. 'Abba' was her first word - the informal version of 'Father' in Aramaic.

At home she told her family she'd chosen to become a Christian, but left out the part about the other language she'd been given.
"You're already a Christian" her father retorted.
"How is that?" she asked.
"You were born in New Zealand," he growled.
"That does not make a person a Christian! You have to be born again," she stated, certain in her new faith.
"Nonsense!" her father yelled, "My cousin said he was a Christian, and got left standing on a hilltop waiting for Christ to come. They said it didn't happen because he wore a coloured sock!"
Shaking her head in bewilderment, she replied; "He joined a cult, I haven't. The ..."
But she was shouted down.
"How dare you? Get out of here. You make me sick. I can't stand you, or your self-righteousness!" he roared.
His anger turned to rage as she tried to get a word in. He flung her so hard against the kitchen door it cracked.
"Do you think God can make your blind grandfather *see*?" he yelled after her as she retreated to her room, "He has *no* power!"

Shut down, she wondered what God had done to make her father so full of venom and hate.
Shaking his head in sadness the Lord spoke the verse from Ephesians 6:4, knowing he wouldn't be heard; *"Fathers, do not exasperate your children; instead, bring them up in the training and instruction of the Lord."*

Curses, confusion and rebuke came with everything Joanna put her hand to. She left school when she turned seventeen, unprepared for what lay ahead. Working life began in a small-town government department. The claims department was a toxic hell-hole, and the abuse and exploitation began immediately.

Her father hadn't allowed her to go to university and so, needing a job she'd asked for the Lord's guidance - never dreaming she'd end up in a horrible office like this. Would it never end? Perhaps it was all she deserved.

Longing for a few words of affirmation and encouragement, she worked hard; but all she got at work was belittlement and bullying. She also copped abuse from angry customers at the counter.
At the bottom of the heap, she asked herself despairingly "Is this all there is?" on the days when she was abused and treated like dirt at home and at work.

"Wasn't life supposed to get better after I got saved?" she asked herself.

As time went by, she began to doubt the King's love for her. "Where are you?" she cried, hearing no answer.

For the next two years she walked in her own strength, until the day came when she was too demoralised and discouraged to continue. Walking off the path, she made her way into the world.

The death

The lost daughter continued on her way without the King. She left home at the age of eighteen and chose her future husband without consulting the Lord. After all, look what happened when she'd asked him to guide her. Thomas, the man she married, was not a believer.

In the year 1980 everything started to break apart. First it was her family and then the following year, her brother. "There is something wrong with my head" her brother Gareth sobbed. "I can't be like Mum …" he added fearfully.

"We'll fix it, we'll fix it" Joanna replied, not knowing where to turn.
Distressed she asked herself, "What can I do?"
"Bring Gareth to me" the Lord urged in response to her anguished question.
Desperate, Joanna called out "Is that really you Lord? Will you save him?"
The Lord replied; *"He that comes to me I will in no wise cast out." John 6:37 (NKJ)*
Joanna could not hear his reply.

Satan mocked her, reminding her of how her brother had laughed at her when she became a Christian.

She could see that her brother was swimming in a river of madness and they were out of options. Love overcame her fear of rejection as she steadied herself to reach for him. It felt like she was trying to save a drowning man.

Joanna stood in front of her brother in the kitchen of their father's farm house.

They were alone; their mother no longer lived at the house and their father had gone away to be with their mother's former best friend.

The divorce of their parents had been hard, but the children understood why the marriage had ended. They weren't stupid; their parent's marriage had been undermined by their mother's manic episodes and their father's bitterness. They knew the affair between their father and their mother's best friend had been the end result of all that unhappiness and selfishness.

What they found hard to accept was the betrayal of their mother. She had few friends, and now she was abandoned by her best friend and husband – two people she'd trusted and believed in. Now they, the children, were caught in the middle with divided loyalties, and they were left to fend for themselves. Often the youngest girls would get off the school bus, find no one waiting, and walk all the way home to stay alone in an empty house.

Cut adrift, they had no-one to confide in. They waited in vain for somebody to care and wondered why no one asked after them.

All they received were lectures from some of their father's relatives up north about "how they should be happy for their father" leaving their mother. They weren't coping, and then their distressed brother grew ill.

Joanna feared her father would be against what she was about to attempt. Overcoming her fear, she looked her brother in the eyes asking; "Gareth, would you like God to help you?"
"Yes" he said, starting to cry.

Joanna made her way back to the Lord, her eyes burning with hope and fear as she carefully guided her sick brother to him for healing. Watching the road for the children, God the Father saw them approach.

He'd been watching the road for a long time.
If only they could see his face, they'd *know* he loved them.

He gave them a message about 'The prodigal son' that day; a story Jesus told about a father waiting for his lost son.

The father had been watching the road, and when his son was still a long way off, he saw him and he ran, his heart full of pity for his son. He threw his arms around his son, saying; *"Let us celebrate with a feast! For this son of mine was dead, but now he is alive; he was lost, but now he has been found." (Luke 15)*

Gareth came to the Lord through the same gate Joanna had found, saying; *"Though my father and mother forsake me, the LORD will receive me." Psalm 27:10.*

His new found faith gave him peace of mind. The fear Joanna felt for him left as he got better. For a year he went from strength to strength.

Now related in the Kingdom as well as by blood, they talked about the Lord often, their eyes shining. Joanna was also getting to know God the Father, although she was hampered by an accusing voice that said "You are only back because of your brother."

The dream of my Father

Gareth got baptised in 1983, to show he was serious about following the Lord. His face was shining, full of light as he came out of the water. Joanna was sorry that his disapproving girlfriend chose to stay in the car rather than support him.

A prophecy was given, but it seemed more a message of reassurance; *"Fear not, for the everlasting arms of the Father are about you, guiding and protecting you. As a Kangaroo keeps its young in its pouch, so will I keep you."*
Joanna frowned. What word was there of his future?

Three weeks later Gareth's mental illness returned with a vengeance. He could not get a diagnosis, even though he checked himself into hospital asking for help. He was abandoned by the medical establishment. They hid the name of his disease and their lack of treatment behind the NZ Privacy Act; a law that dictated mental health sufferers not be told the name of their illness. The family only found at the inquest that the disease was called schizophrenia, the medical name for 'confusion'.

After Gareth's death Joanna found a poem in his room;

"Sing a song of madness,
Sitting on his bike,
Topping off at ninety,
Heading down the pike.
But a hundred miles away from home,
Back he had to hike,
Because suddenly it hit him,
He'd left without his bike."

Joanna had grown increasingly concerned seeing her brother's anguish as he grappled with his confused mental state. She warned her parents and anyone who would listen that she feared he'd do harm to himself. Her worst fears were realised.

After his death she learned Gareth was denied treatment at the new medical facility that had just been built.

He'd pinned all his hopes on getting help there. The doctor wrote him a script for pills instead, which he just sat and stared at for hours. Left without hope he chose to die rather than live afflicted by mental illness. At the instant the gun went off the Lord went to get their father who was still asleep at his house.

In his mercy, the Lord allowed this stubborn and unbelieving sheep farmer to accompany his son on his final journey; allowing him right up to the Gate of his Kingdom so he could say goodbye.

Sobbing, her father related his dream;

"We're in the car, Sylvia, Gareth and I. We drove, until we came to a tunnel with some spikes at the entrance. We couldn't drive through so Sylvia stayed in the car, while Gareth and I walked through the tunnel. We walked up a hill to a gate. Through the gate was the most beautiful land I have ever seen; and I never dream in colour. Gareth walked through the gate and turned to me. He looked so happy, his face was radiant."
Gareth said, "You can't go any further. We have to say goodbye now."

The dream ended with the phone ringing to tell me he'd gone."

The dream was like a life raft in an ocean of grief for the shipwrecked family. About to drown, Joanna clung to it.

"It's the Church that did this," Gareth's girlfriend accused, and Joanna cried again.

"Think of your sisters" her husband said, uncomfortable with her grief. Joanna retreated from him in anguish, her eyes swollen shut from crying.

The day after her brother's death Joanna was set upon by the aunt who'd shut her down as a child, the one who'd not allowed her to cry when her grandparents left. Believing that Joanna was attacking her brother, she got Joanna alone in her old room at her father's house.

"Stop feeling sorry for yourself," she chided, castigating Joanna for 'self-pity' before getting onto her favourite subject - her brother's divorce. "Your father needs to be happy ..." she lectured Joanna.

"Don't tell me how to feel! Did you ever stop to consider us?" Joanna sobbed in the face of her aunt's insensitivity. Shocked, she retreated to the same barren place inside herself that she went to when hounded by her mother.

This aunt identified herself as a Christian.
"The Father does not love you," Satan told her.
Joanna was afraid he was right.

The Lord did his best to comfort Joanna, reminding her of the dream he'd given her father and the servant he'd sent her the day before, on the morning of her brother's death. Eventually the room emptied out, leaving Joanna alone on the sofa.

She became aware of a woman praying for her in an unknown tongue.
"Who are you?" she asked.
"I am from the neighbourhood" the woman replied, her presence reassuring Joanna that God had not abandoned her.

Before the year was out, he would move her to a better and kinder place. Eight months later, Joanna started a new life in Sydney.

The place of healing

In the wake of her brother's death and in another country, Joanna learned about her past. At home in her Sydney apartment, she settled down to read, absorbed in the book her half-English, half-German father had given her of his German family history. She studied the photo of her great-great grandparents Wilhelm and Anna, glad to see what they looked like. Before this they'd been invisible; separated by a gulf of time, language and culture.

Included in the book were some letters from Anna to her children. *"Ich bete zu den lieben Vater und rufe Abba wie ein Kind,"* she'd written.
"I pray to the dear Father and call Abba as a child," Joanna read the translation.

A feeling of peace and deep comfort washed over her at the words Anna spoke about the Father. It replaced some of the weariness and loneliness she felt. Joanna experienced a feeling of kinship at the knowledge Anna had been a believer.
This woman would have rejoiced in the salvation of her and her brother.

Joanna thought about the word 'Abba'. The death of her brother and attack of her aunt had put deep dents in her faith. She did not call the Father 'Abba', even though the Lord in his mercy had given her a place to heal in Australia, where her husband's family had set up a business in Sydney's south west.

When she arrived in Sydney at the end of 1983, she loved her new life and the Australians instantly. Sydney was the right place for her; a vibrant, positive place without the constrictions of life in small town New Zealand. People gave her a chance, and she quickly advanced at work. She could see the open sky, the promise and the possibilities - but she was trapped, tethered by her husband and his family. They'd bought their small-town mentality with them and did not adapt to Sydney. She tried to be happy with them but it felt like she was only tolerated for the sake of her husband Thomas. It didn't matter that while the business was getting established, she often worked for them for no pay in the factory on the weekends.

The family worked together and socialised together. The word 'together' meant husband and family, not husband and wife. She felt they were all being controlled by their father in law's wishes.

The threat to go back to their old town in New Zealand hung over her head. It was always there. She felt stifled and trapped, and wanted to scream *"No!"* when the family talked about "going home."
"Can't we stay here?" she asked her husband in anguish.
"No. Do you think I want to be here?" Thomas shot back.

Her mind flashed back to her childhood. She was in the cowshed with her grandmother at Napier. "Gran, you're not going to move, are you?" she'd asked anxiously, after hearing her grandmother say something about leaving Napier.
"Why are you asking me that? Do you think I want to be here?" her grandmother had snapped. Her child's world crumbled. What was she going to do without her? Afterwards, staring blankly at the cowshed wall, all she could see were wings. She drew a picture of a bird on the cowshed wall where her grandmother had uttered her bitter words.

Suddenly there was a flash of white wings as a light blue budgie flew into their apartment. He'd flown in seeking shelter from a group of big black Currawong birds who were attacking him. The bird arrived on Valentine's Day.

"Seek your happiness in me, and I will grant your heart's desire" *(Psalm 37:3)* the Lord wrote.

Every good and perfect gift is from above, coming down from the Father, but the Father's gift went unnoticed. Joanna just thought she was really lucky.

"I'll be there for you," Joanna promised the bird as he trustingly sat on her hand. She could feel his heart beating against her finger. Joanna loved the delightful little character from the start and soon the little bird learned to talk. The cage door was left open so he could fly around the flat at will. He had as much freedom as she could give him. She knew what it felt like to be caged.

The door to Joanna's own cage was firmly shut after four years, when Thomas and his family made the decision to return to New Zealand that she'd been dreading. There was no discussion in the matter as Joanna was not taken into account.

She lived a life ruled by other people's agendas. In her life she desired fairness and a win-win outcome, but her needs weren't considered. "You don't matter" she'd learned. It led to situations like this where she didn't have a choice about where to live or where to work.

Believing she had no say, she caved in to her husband and his family's wishes. It tore her heart out to have to leave. She lost everything in order to keep them happy; her refuge, her place in the world, her career, her identity, her friends, and her new found sense of security and belonging.

Joanna was devastated. Against her will, she walked out of Wellington airport clutching her little bird in his cage, stricken at being back in New Zealand. It was like a death.

Thomas, who'd returned to New Zealand two months earlier, met her at the airport. He couldn't bear her sobs and asked her to stop, so she forced herself to swallow her grief whole. It was indigestible. After stopping at her father's place where her sisters had gathered to welcome her back, she ate her meal and threw it back up.

At the end of 1987, Joanna returned to a small town devoid of friends and career prospects. Her sisters and friends had all left in the intervening years. Only Joanna's mother and second husband Barry were still there.

When her mother knew she was coming back she interfered in Joanna's life by going around the real estate agents looking for houses on her behalf; just as she'd done with employers when Joanna was a teenager looking for a job. Joanna felt embarrassed and crushed, experiencing the same feelings she'd had as a child.

A simple man of low intelligence, Barry didn't mind her mother's craziness. In fact, when she went high - so did he. He was never going to bring any correction because he loved it when her mother was like that. A fool spreading slander, he enjoyed a good gossip.

They fed off Joanna by running her down to others, verbally attacking her, borrowing money they didn't intend to repay, and turning up at her house when they weren't welcome.

She was put through hell. It mattered, but Joanna felt powerless. She felt preyed upon.

Resentful and broken hearted, Joanna hid behind a mask in the years that followed. It seemed everything within her had died except for grief. Putting a good face on her marriage she did all that was expected and demanded, keeping up appearances and going through the motions. She was good at that. What she had not been trained to do was spot a liar.

Chapter Two

Soon after their first child was born in 1989, Joanna's husband began working overseas. She was left on her own with her baby son for months at a time. A baby girl followed 18 months later, and then they were on their own again. "Daddy works" was her daughter's first sentence.

In 1992 she met a man she was later to call 'Silver-tongue' while doing a programming paper at the local college. He wormed his way into her home after suggesting they study together. Joanna was quickly marked out as a source of narcissistic supply.

"Your husband should have put you first. I would," Silver-tongue told Joanna earnestly, licking his lips and baiting the hook after finding out why she no longer lived in Sydney. Joanna had a crying need, although hidden and unacknowledged, for a man who would put her first in his life. He could see it.

Disguised as Prince Charming, he asked her a lot of questions and carefully listened, repeating her answers to show Joanna she was being actively listened to. He cleverly discerned her need and spoke into all the areas of neglect, giving her a vision of what life could be ... if she would only trust herself to him.

"I love you. I've never felt this way about *anybody*," he declared after a few weeks.

He used the word 'love' like a charm to get what he wanted. Although he felt love for himself, that feeling didn't extend to other people.

He was a parasite who needed admiration, and in order to get it he had to *pretend* to love others – until he had them under his control.

He knew the words that would hook women in ... words like commitment, love, and marriage. These words were skilfully and cynically employed on Joanna. He was very persuasive.

Mimicking her gestures and making solid eye contact, he made sure his hand didn't stray across his mouth and his nose as he lied; "Trust me, Joanna. You're special. I know you don't want to be here, but I'm glad you are. I'll make it up to you if you let me. You're the woman I've been looking for all my life. I want to make a commitment to you. I want to make up for everything you've lost coming back to New Zealand. I want to marry you," he promised earnestly, his expression serious.

"How can you marry me when we're already married to other people?" Joanna asked.

"She's not what I want," he said sadly, painting a picture of an unhappy wife who would leave him as soon as he found someone else. "We had to get married because she got pregnant. We're only together for the kids, and she wants to leave. The marriage has been over for a long time" he explained.

Joanna believed him, seeing him like her father. It seemed they were in a similar situation, and her father "deserved to be happy." Didn't she deserve to be happy too?

Reluctantly and against her will Joanna fell for 'Prince Charming', without realising the nastiness that lurked just under the charm.

Abusive, boastful, treacherous, conceited, and a lover of himself; he was exactly the type of person the Bible warned about in Timothy 3:1-9, where there would be terrible times in the last days. *"Have nothing to do with such people,"* God warned.

Unmindful of the warning in the Bible, Joanna took him at face value. Presenting himself as an alpha male, Silver-tongue basked in her admiration.

Silver-Tongue quickly noted that Joanna responded to approval, and he showered her with words of affirmation. Having never been given any praise until she worked in Australia, Joanna believed he was giving her back some of the things she'd lost. For the first time in her life, she allowed herself to believe *she* mattered.

"*You* deserve to be happy" Silver-tongue said, promising her the world. Her heart soared on the strength of his promises.

There is a proverb in the Bible that says *"Fervent lips with a wicked heart are like earthenware covered with silver dross." Proverbs 26:23 (NKJ)*

Silver-tongue would soon earn his name from his words … cheap, insincere words uttered with intense emotion; words that were rubbish wrapped in silver dross. His mouth was an open grave. Words cost him nothing. The people who paid were the women he conned and their families. His extravagant lies cost Joanna everything.

Joanna moved to a two storey flat they called "The Brown House" where she lived alone. She refused to leave her children and move straight in with Silver-tongue as he wanted.

Her new neighbourhood was in an old area of town the locals called 'Poverty Flats'. The Brown House was a far cry from the house she owned - a three-story pole house built into the side of a hill with a beautiful view of Mount Ruapehu, an active Volcano.

Thomas was still living in the marital property, rent free. He was used to getting the lion's share of everything.

Joanna had one close friend who'd moved back to the town, or at least she thought she did. Thomas was secretly having an affair with her, but he blamed Joanna for leaving. Thomas got his own way through guilt trips, and Joanna had been brought up to accept blame. Throughout their marriage, he'd treated her as a scapegoat.
Crushed and guilt-ridden, Joanna accepted the victim role without question.

She unhappily agreed she was responsible for the split and moved out, letting him have everything. All she wanted was her freedom. The only thing Joanna would not give up was the children. It was best to keep him happy for the children's sake. Whenever he was home, they shared custody of the children who were then just two and three years old.

Contact

Silver-tongue's mask of charm began to slip by Christmas of 1993 after waiting six months for Joanna to move in to his house. His original plan was for Joanna to move in with him earlier in the year, as soon as he'd evicted his wife. He thought he'd put an ad in the paper as soon as his bed was empty, seeking a housekeeper to look after his young family. Joanna would answer the ad, move in to his house and present the wife and family with a "fait accompli".

That was Plan A.

Joanna thought the idea sucked and refused to usurp her.

"No one would buy that - and what would your wife do if I answered the door? It's her house as well. Get someone else to mind your children if your wife isn't going to take them!" she told him, suggesting they wait six months before living together. Warning bells should have flashed then but they didn't. Joanna was used to selfish and irrational people. She didn't know she deserved any better.

Angry that Joanna hadn't followed his plan, Silver-tongue devised another course of action, careful to hide his narcissistic anger.

For the last six months, his wife slept at her own place, but came back during the day to look after the children. Joanna refused to be the one to change that. She waited for him to move out himself or do something to resolve the stalemate, unaware of how selfish he was; unaware that he did not intend to split the marital property or let his wife take the children.

After growing impatient waiting for Joanna to move in, he'd gone to Plan B, allowing his wife to move back home. He decided he would live with his wife and see Joanna on the side. He'd done that before and his wife was used to it.

He'd introduce the idea to Joanna bit by bit and dress it up so she'd accept it. To start with, he concocted a story about his wife staying in the family home while her flat was being painted. It was the month of Christmas, and he knew Joanna was distracted by her father's illness, which gave him an advantage.

Joanna's father had just been diagnosed with inoperable bowel cancer, and to add to her grief her beloved pet bird died of cancer at the same time. "Are you calling me a liar?" he challenged Joanna when she questioned the timing. He could see the warning bells were flashing in her mind. His challenge worked, but he wouldn't be able to employ it again, because he was a liar through and through. Joanna backed off, bewildered and bereft.

A week later he tried to manipulate Joanna into accepting his wife being back, by telling her a philosophical story about a traveller and a village. The village was the same village, even though the traveller approached it from two different directions. "I'm asking for your trust," he said as he finished his little homily.

"I am not going to put up with this," Joanna warned. "Let's get through Christmas," Silver-tongue replied, putting her off. He did the same thing at New Year, putting her off again.

Angry that she wasn't going to go for Plan B, he got nasty when his attempts at manipulating her failed. She deserved Plan B because she didn't follow Plan A.

Joanna grieved the loss of Prince Charming - but could not bring herself to believe the ugliness she'd glimpsed beneath the mask. He always had a rational explanation for his behaviour.

Somehow Joanna got through Christmas, but New Year was another thing. She couldn't sleep and suffered a panic attack. The day after New Year she sat upstairs on her bed, wondering if she was being betrayed by the man she loved. Where was he? She had been alone for six months now, waiting for him, and she missed her home. How could she go on coping with all the loss?

In desperation she called out to the Lord, seeking forgiveness. This was her last resort. She reasoned he could only say no.

After all, what else did she have to lose?

Joanna's sister Christen had come to the Lord after their brother's death; and had sent a Bible with a book of daily scripture readings. The books lay beside her on the bed. The Lord heard the *'SOS'*.

Eyeing Joanna intently, he willed her to turn to him. Although she could not see or hear him, he wanted her to listen. His voice came very soft and quiet; "Turn off the radio."

Thinking the voice was her own, she did as she was told, wishing with all her heart she was not alone.

"Fear not, for I AM here," he said speaking very softly into her mind in the silence of the room.
"Come to me, you who are heavily laden," he added.

As Joanna listened, she suddenly got a glimpse of him, as a vision flashed into her mind of a Father looking down at his baby. A look of deep tenderness was on the face of the Father, as he held the baby against his cheek.

The quiet words began again ... "Child, do you see that baby the father is holding? Although he's holding her, she can't see him, for her eyes can't yet focus."

Joanna nodded.

"You are that baby," he said, as his voice roughened with emotion; "There are so many things I want to show you, but you cannot yet see ..."

Sighing, she leafed through the book of daily Bible readings, wishing the vision was real instead of her just trying to comfort herself. How could he love her?
Finding the word for that day from Hosea 11, she started to read.

"When you were a child, I loved you, and I called you out of Egypt as my daughter. But the more I called to you, the more you turned away from me. My people sacrificed to Baal; they burned incense to idols.

Yet I was the one who taught them to walk. I took my people up in their arms, but they did not acknowledge that I took care of them. I drew them to me with affection and love. I picked them up and held them to my cheek; I bent down to them and fed them ..."

Joanna shook and the Bible slid from her hands, as the Father explained how her people had turned away from him. When she reached the part where he held his children to his cheek, he saw her tears fall on the page.
"How can I give you up?" he cried; *"How can I abandon you? My heart will not let me do it! My love for you is too strong. All my compassion is aroused. I will not come to you in anger."*

Joy and wonder ran as deep as the grief, and she started to sob. How could it be? The Bible reading from Hosea confirmed the vision she'd just been given about the love of the Father. It was a miracle.

Comforted, Joanna wiped her eyes and raised her head.
Aware of him, she said "I can hear you!"

The Father smiled.

The Princess

The next morning the Bible beckoned to her. Picking it up, it fell open in the middle of the book, at Psalm 119:18-19 (NIV). *"Open my eyes that I may see wonderful things in your word. I am a stranger on the earth; do not hide your commands from me,"* she read aloud, wondering about the things he wanted to show her that she could not yet see.

Smiling at her first attempt at speaking to him through his word, the Lord replied as he directed her to another page; *"When you call, I will answer, I will show you great and marvellous things, of which you know not." (Jeremiah 33:3)*

Joanna learned that the Lord always confirmed his word. Later in the day she saw a movie every little girl would love. Accompanied by her best friend Nerida, they took their children to see Aladdin. The film resonated with her. At the scene where Aladdin and Jasmine were together singing "A whole new world", Joanna heard the Lord call her a Princess, telling her he would show her the world. At the scene where they soared into the sky, leaving Egypt behind them singing "A whole new world ..." the princess in Joanna awoke.

In her happiness Joanna wanted to tell Nerida that she'd heard the Lord speak for the very first time. Nerida had given up on the Lord in her teenage years and displeased, she cut Joanna off. Not wanting to alienate her friend, Joanna closed her mouth and kept silent about the Lord after that. Joanna feared Nerida would not like the princess.

Being able to speak with God changed everything for Joanna. She treasured his words in her heart. Uncomfortable at calling God "Father", Joanna called him "Lord".

"What should I do about Silver-tongue?" Joanna asked the Lord as she struggled through the months of 1994.

Silver-tongue was still in her life. He'd been sleeping at his parent's place since the beginning of the year in order to keep Joanna - but she no longer trusted him, and he only did the bare minimum to keep the 'relationship' going.

The charm offensive was over. He'd gone to work on her, convincing her that she was only being treated as she deserved. After idealising her he was now tearing her apart, piece by piece.

"Leave him" the Lord replied.

Although Joanna wanted to, she couldn't.
"I want to, but God help me, I can't. Please forgive me, and help me. I can't do this on my own," Joanna replied.

"I know," he replied. He would have to walk her through this.

The gift of the Shepherd

For endless winter days, Joanna wearily trudged through the Valley of the Shadow of death. Her father's house lay in that valley. He died in the winter of 1994. For Joanna, it was a dark place where she did not laugh and she did not smile.

Joanna remembered the final conversation she had with her father, the day before he died. He could see a future for her without Silver-Tongue and his machinations. It was the first time in her life he'd affirmed her.

He said "I'm sorry I never let you go to university. I was wrong. But keep studying for your computer qualification, and look after the children. I'm sorry I won't see them grow up. I know you'll do well in life. Even though you're struggling right now, you *will* work it out. I believe in you."

In saying that, he said everything.

Today, she was alone, as usual. Tired and drained, Joanna stood by the fire inside in her father's house trying to get warm.

They'd gone there at his wife's request for the sad task of sorting out his belongings. She tried not to look at her father's empty chair.

The shepherd's staff stood near the chair, unnoticed in the corner of the room where it had been left leaning since the day of her Father's death.
"One of you girls can take that," Sylvia his widow said, suddenly noticing the staff.
Joanna recognised it.
"That's my old crook" she remarked, surprised. She thought it had been left on the farm.
"It was down in his workshop," Sylvia said. "He'd made it down there the other day, but was too weak to walk back up the path. I

found him leaning on it, unable to move. It's yours, so please take it."

They gave her his car. As she got the engine running, a thin stream of water shot out of the radiator, landing in an arc on the concrete in front of her sisters. Joanna sighed and cracked an egg into the radiator water, praying it would hold until she could get the leak fixed.

She realised her father had been too ill to maintain the vehicle, even though he'd been a mechanic by trade. His stuff was still in the car; the paperback he'd been reading was face down on the seat where he'd left it. Joanna laid the crook in the back of the car and concentrated on getting the neglected vehicle home.

At home she put the crook in the corner of the room and cried. It was more than she could cope with. Just as it had at her father's house, the humble crook stayed leaning against the wall unnoticed, until the Lord came to comfort her. Joanna's tear-filled eyes were drawn to the staff. She noticed it had been varnished. Mindful of the care taken in its preservation, she asked "Does this crook have some significance?"
The Lord replied, giving her some dates, and a number;
"From the day you left Napier on the 4th day of August 1971, to the day of your Father's death on the 4th day of August 1994, 23 years were written in my book. When your father leaned on the staff, I was there.
Now the time for your father has ended, and you will go on. Read Psalm 23. It will be familiar to you."
Opening the Bible, Joanna read about the Lord who was a Shepherd. She smiled, carried back to the place where she had first encountered him in the valley. She could see the hills, the sheep, the creek and the quiet pool by the willows.
"That was *you*, wasn't it?" she asked.
He nodded.

Her eyes lingered on the crook, the shepherd's staff. Taking it in her hands, she ran her fingers over the smooth wood, remembering. The staff had come back to her as a great gift from the Shepherd; and it comforted her.

Wiping her eyes she said; *"Even though I walk through the valley of the shadow of death, I will fear no evil; for you are with me; your rod and staff comfort me."* Psalm 23

Treasuring the gift of the staff and his word, she added, *"I rejoice at your word, as one who finds great treasure." (Psalm 119:162)*

The Lord smiled. *The Kingdom of Heaven is like treasure buried in a field.* She'd had to go through the grief to find the gift. "*Blessed are those who mourn, for they shall be comforted," Matthew 5:4 (NIV)* he promised.

The word at the levelled hill

Now that Joanna had contact with the Lord she was reading his word with new eyes. It became personal. Not long after her journey through the Valley of Shadow he prepared her for the next stage of the journey;

"I will lead you by ways you have not known, along unfamiliar paths I will guide you; I will turn the darkness into light before you and make the rough places smooth. These are the things I will do; I will not forsake you.

I myself will prepare your way, leveling mountains and hills. I will go before you, and make the crooked places straight: I will break in pieces the gates of bronze, and cut asunder the bars of iron." (Isaiah 42:9-16, 45:2)

On a hot summer evening in January 1995, Joanna stopped for the night at her aunt's farm, on her way back home from her Gran's 90th birthday in Northland. After tea they stood on the balcony overlooking the farmland of the King Country. The evening shadows folded into the rolling hills that sprawled out towards Otorohanga and the old volcanic cone of Mount Kakepuku.

The land had its secret places for underneath the hills were caves that the Maori called 'tomo'. As they enjoyed the warmth of the early evening sun, they talked of the farm.

"Do you see that hill over there?" asked her aunt, the one who had read her Bible stories at bed time, as she pointed at a levelled hill. "We weren't able to make the track over it, or around it, so we levelled the hill top."

Later when Joanna came into his presence, the Lord said, "I know you saw the sign of the levelled hill."
Nodding, Joanna replied "You will prepare my way, levelling mountains and hills."

"Yes" he replied; "From now on, I will confirm my word by the signs that accompany it. I want you to keep a record of those signs."
Joanna nodded her assent.
"Here are your directions," the Lord said as he opened up his word; *"Set up signposts, make landmarks; set your heart toward the highway, the way in which you take. Turn back, O virgin of Israel, turn back to these your cities. How long will you gad about, backsliding daughter?*
For the LORD has created a new thing in the earth— a woman shall encompass a man." Jeremiah 31:21-22 (NKJ);

Joanna didn't much like the part about "backsliding" or "gadding about", but thought it best not to go there with the Lord.

Baffled at his instructions, she questioned him; "Your directions are as mysterious as the road. What do you mean by "turn back to these your cities?" Do you mean turn back to Sydney, Wanganui, or even Napier? What do you mean by the words 'a woman shall encompass a man,' or 'a woman shall circle a man?'"

"Set your heart toward the highway," the Lord answered; "The way will become clear from the road you mark."

Driving back home through the King country Joanna thought about the road signs as they flashed by. In the natural it was easy, but the road to the Kingdom of God was a hidden road, a narrow road called "The Way." It was the only road with signs and the Lord wanted her to watch for them. Would she be able to see the signs?

As she joined the King's highway heading south Joanna wondered if she would travel the road alone as she was doing now.

"Will Silver-tongue find the road?" she asked.

"The road is narrow and difficult to find. Only those who seek the Kingdom of God find it," the Lord answered.
"What signs will I be given?" she asked.

"You will know the signs when you see them. They will agree with my word," he explained.

"How can I follow a road that I cannot see?" she wondered.

"There will be others on the road who will guide you at different places," he replied, adding;
"Although the Lord gives you the bread of adversity and the water of affliction, your teachers will be hidden no more; with your own eyes you will see them. Whether you turn to the right or to the left, your ears will hear a voice behind you, saying, "This is the way; walk in it." Isaiah 30:20-21 (NIV)

Coal under pressure

Joanna went back to college in 1994, studying part time for a career she planned once the children were in school. The qualification she aimed for formed the first year of a degree in Computer Science.

The thought of a career in her chosen field brought her hope in an otherwise desolate landscape. She thought of the college as her safe place.

Unfortunately, Silver-tongue enrolled for the same papers. He kept a jealous eye on her, making caustic remarks if she chatted to any of the men at break time while watching the second-year students play hacky-sack.

One of the second-year students was a lean man in his thirties with a handsome, boyish face and greying hair. He was in the background. Silver-tongue demanded all of her attention.

Joanna had to do a compulsory paper called 'Interpersonal Skills' and part of it dealt with stress. They were given a weighted list of all the things that caused stress; separation or divorce, moving house, death, relationship problems. Joanna ticked off the list she was studying. It was a real eye opener. How was she even functioning? The children and the hope of a career kept her going.

Silver-tongue caused the most stress. He ate with his wife and kids, visited her at night and slept at his parent's. He'd created a triangle for himself that she hated being part of. For the life of her she couldn't figure out when and how she'd even agreed to it.

Besides him, her ex-husband and her mother caused equal amounts of stress and made life hell. Divorce and another house move loomed large on the horizon. There seemed to be no end to the grief.

The next day she told her friend Eve, an attractive and graceful blonde about the stress. They were feeding the deer at the Deer Park, over the road from where Eve lived. Eve found it interesting as she was going through her own trials.

Sticking some stale bread through the fence, she turned to Joanna saying "Did you know that coal under pressure forms a diamond?"

Glancing at the bare finger on her left-hand Joanna said wryly; "It had better be a pretty big diamond!"
Silver-tongue had promised her a ring last Christmas. Still waiting and believing for it, Joanna had yet to discover that Silver-tongue used false promises as another means to stay in control.

The Riddler

Each time Joanna depended on Silver-Tongue for something, it was like eating with a cavity or walking with an injury.

It reminded her of the proverb; *'Like a broken tooth or a lame foot is reliance on the unfaithful in a time of trouble.' Proverbs 25:19 (NIV)*

She'd pick herself up after being let down because of the promises he made and his assertions that he was the 'right man' for her.

He dismissed her by saying "Most women would love the way you're being treated."

Negated, Joanna felt deeply resentful, but put up with it because of her low self-esteem. He got away with neglect and abuse because she was used to it, and it was to his advantage if he could convince her she deserved it.

Joanna didn't know what a healthy relationship looked like, but she wanted to learn. She tried counselling in the year her father died, hoping to get heard - but she was no match for Silver-tongue.

Silver-tongue regarded counselling as a contest he was going to win. He expertly twisted things in order to get control, or he'd undermine her by saying "I never said that." Words, sentences and phrases were taken out of context, changed in his favour and thrown back at Joanna like darts. He made her look irrational, and crazy. It was a never-ending mind game. Joanna would end up in tears. Forced to defend herself, nothing got resolved.

The counsellor did not see the contempt, the curl of his lip, or the sneering look. She only saw a caring, understanding, reasonable man who cared deeply for an angry and tearful woman; a woman who wasn't making any sense.

Joanna could see she wasn't being listened to, and she was in despair - stuck in the triangle Silver-tongue had created. That was the biggest issue, because he said she was angry all the time – and he had no intention of moving the 'relationship' on with an angry woman. Silver-tongue brought up her anger at counselling.

In a final appeal, Joanna angrily drew the triangle she'd been manipulated into on the whiteboard, crying "Of course I'm angry. Is this reasonable, sane or normal? Do other women put up with this? I need to know!"

Silver-tongue looked at the counsellor helplessly with tears in his eyes. The counsellor noticed. "Joanna, swap seats with him" she said dismissively. Joanna slumped in her chair; her head bowed in defeat. Couldn't the counsellor see what he was doing? Why wasn't she being listened to?

When Joanna had first seen the counsellor alone, the woman had been on her side! She'd been shown a circle that demonstrated domestic violence and given sound advice. Relieved at being heard at last, Joanna believed there would be a way out. Her relief was short lived. After meeting Silver-Tongue alone, the counsellor's attitude towards her changed. What on earth had he said?

Joanna realised later that Silver-Tongue would have told the counsellor all about her mother and brother's mental illness. Of course he would have – and it would have been an easy matter to paint her with the same brush while she was grieving for her father. And he made sure she turned up at counselling incoherent by adding a few nasty and well-timed verbal attacks just before the sessions. It worked a charm and brought her to counselling distraught.

Counselling had been her first effort at getting help. Now she didn't know what to do.

Silver-Tongue was triumphant. He'd won. In his arrogance and pride, he did not believe Joanna would ever get free of him – but she told him to go away and not come back.

After waiting a few days, he manipulated her into trying a different counsellor, with promises that he loved her and he would change.

Silver-Tongue was an excellent player of the blame game. After she'd taken him back, he tried very hard to get Joanna to accept that *she* was the source of the problems - and for a while he succeeded, because she had not been heard or believed by the first counsellor.

Joanna didn't know the new counsellor was from a mental health agency. Silver-tongue hid that well. He'd been given his card by the former counsellor; a useful fool, who in siding with him had become Joanna's judge – never realising how she'd been lied to, conned, manipulated and tricked.

Unaware of the true nature of the counselling or of what had transpired behind her back; Joanna tried again - because the new counsellor said he knew the Lord. But the guidance Joanna hoped for was not forthcoming. She dubbed the new counsellor "the Riddler" as he spoke in riddles.

"The way out of this is the same way you went in," the Riddler said, leading her into a bewildering maze.

The 1995 the Riddler did tell her one useful thing. "Tell a story, and then explain," he said, after she complained that she wasn't being heard or helped.

In the telling of her first story about a dragon, a Prince and a King, Joanna suddenly found herself in another world; a Kingdom. She had come into the story after writing about going through a dragon's cave.

Joanna looked around her. She could not see very far. It was foggy, and the land was shrouded in mist.

Bewildered and lost, Joanna sought the King; "Lord, I wanted to get out of Silver-tongue's triangle; but when I went for help, I was accused of being mentally ill, and now I've been led into a maze. I'm not getting the help I need. I need to get to a place where I can feel happy and be safe."

The Lord answered; "If you seek first my Kingdom and my righteousness, you will find the way." "How do I do that?" she asked, wanting a tangible course of action.

"The Kingdom of God is within you. Ask, and you shall receive. Seek, and you shall find. Knock and the door will be opened to you," he replied.

Joanna sighed, thinking about the road she'd started to travel.

The last place she'd got any direction was at the levelled hill. Remembering that the Lord had told her to put up road signs and guideposts and take note of the highway, she decided to continue with the story. It would be useful for recording the signs and guideposts, and she could use it as a map to follow the road.

The Mighty Counsellor

At first, the daily grind, the tyranny of the immediate and the pressing issues of real-life kept Joanna from seeking the Kingdom. She moved from her two storied house to a bigger house in a quiet little lane surrounded by hills and trees. In that tranquil spot she hoped life would get better.

Silver-tongue continued to spend the weekends and days off at his place. He joined her only when the moon appeared, and disappeared when the sun rose. He would not even share the food from her table. The charm turned to nastiness when she confronted him about turning up late at night, or questioned his behaviour. He was like a stray dog; *"They return at evening, snarling like dogs, and prowl about the city." Psalm 59:6 (NIV)*

Silver-tongue kept up his blame game. Joanna would never get anywhere while she was trying to defend herself, and it played into his hands. He always spoke quietly and she could not keep from yelling. It was easy to make her cry. If he was in a foul mood, he'd play a mind game and watch the tears turn to rage.

Smirking at her distress, he'd point out how irrational she was. Kept in constant turmoil, Joanna was too upset and devastated to see how he was pulling the strings.

When she tried to please him, he hit her with a devastating club of disapproval. After being belittled and put down for so long, Joanna believed him when he showed her why she was 'not worthy' of love. The anger and injustice she felt built behind a dam of tears she dared not let go of.

"Take authority over your feelings," the Riddler told Joanna. Joanna didn't know how, or what he even meant. How could she own something she wasn't allowed to have? She gave up on him.

The King wanted to help. Although Joanna could now hear him, it hadn't sunk in that she was his daughter, or the worth that came from that. Determined to honour his promises he worked hard at gaining her trust. Knowing she needed to learn his ways, he began by teaching her about righteousness.

"When I return," he said; "the government will be on my shoulders. *And I will be called 'Wonderful Counsellor', 'Mighty God', 'Everlasting Father', and Prince of Peace ..." (Isaiah 9:6)*

With her ears pricking up at the title of 'Wonderful Counsellor,' Joanna made her appeal.

"The counsellors have failed me. No help can be found from them after they listen to Silver-tongue; only harm. They're useless, without any discernment. I know you are not like them and you can see what is going on. Will *you* counsel me?"

"I will," the King replied, after waiting for her to ask. Silver-tongue would not be able to turn *him* against her.

"Follow me" he said. Joanna followed the King to a castle. He led her across the keep into the castle armoury.

Looking out the window, she saw a large flag flying in the wind, with a golden lion emblazoned on a sapphire background.

On the wall there was a large sign that said, *"Put on all the armour that God gives you, so that you will be able to stand up against the Devil's evil tricks. For we are not fighting against human beings, but against the wicked spiritual forces in the heavenly world, the rulers, authorities, and cosmic powers of this dark age. So put on God's armour now!*

Then when the evil day comes, you will be able to resist the enemy's attacks; and after fighting to the end, you will still hold your ground." Ephesians 6:11-13 (GNT)

The words seemed to glow with hidden power.

Dropping a load of armour at her feet, the King explained how her anger was being exploited. He said; *"If you cannot control your anger, you are as helpless as a city without walls, open to attack." Proverbs 25:28 (GNT)*

Handing her a mighty sword, he said "Be careful with that. It's the Sword of the Spirit. Go smote the dragon, not the man you regard as a prince."

In the world outside the Kingdom the sword was the Bible, a much-maligned book that had been dismissed and ignored for centuries. It sat unused on many a dusty bookshelf. How could this be a weapon?

Shaking her head in puzzlement Joanna asked, "Seriously, how can this be a sword?"

"Read my word," he smiled; "Read it, remember it, and repeat it. Practise the three 'r's. I will bring the word to mind when you need it. Use my word and watch what happens!"

"Are the three r's like an-*RRR*?" she asked, like a kitten trying to roar. The King laughed, and in his laughter she heard the roar of a lion; a roar that would one day shake the world.

The Sword of the Spirit

"You will never amount to anything," Silver-tongue snarled, in a foul mood because Joanna had beaten him in an exam. He'd just got out of his car and was ready to lash her with his tongue. "*RRR*" Joanna thought, reaching for her sword. Suddenly the Lord's word flashed into her mind, and the princess within picked it up and ran with it.

"You curse, but the Lord will bless!" she parried.

Silver-tongue was left speechless. His words always found their mark. If his aim was really good Joanna would be left an abused and snivelling wreck. He expected her to cry and attempt to defend herself. Suddenly he glimpsed a self-confident woman who would not need his approval. He'd just met the princess and he didn't like her. Silver-Tongue backed off, the princess looked satisfied, and the King smiled. She'd get the blessing and he'd get the bluster.

In the Kingdom, the Princess held the King's steady gaze as she studied the sword. Double edged, it shone with light.

The King said; *"For the word of God is living and active. Sharper than any double-edged sword, it penetrates even to dividing soul and spirit, joints and marrow; it judges the thoughts and attitudes of the heart." Hebrews 4:12 (NKJ)*

It was the only offensive weapon he gave her. He told her it would cut right through to where the soul and spirit met, but it could not be used to attack people.

The sword impressed Joanna with its power, but she worried about getting the words in time. She knew Silver-tongue or the dragon would be back for a counter attack. If she got angry enough, they'd gain control.

Joanna told the King that she just wasn't strong enough to pick up the mighty sword; and the dragon often took the appearance of the man she regarded as a prince.

She asked the Lord, "Which one would I strike?"

"Learn from my Word and I will give you the gift of distinguishing between spirits," the King promised. She would be given the ability to see the dragon, and with practise she'd develop the strength and wisdom to wield the sword correctly.

The time for anger came again. Silver-tongue had asked her to make his lunches.

Looking at him with hatred Joanna responded; "What a cheek. Why are you even asking for that again? I did that for months until I asked for the money for YOUR corn-beef, which you refused to give me."

"I wanted to treat you like a wife," he replied, looking entitled and aggrieved.

Disgusted, Joanna looked at his beautifully pressed business shirt. "Who ironed your shirt?"

"My wife," Silver-tongue replied, sensing trouble.

"Oh, I see. So, what is getting her to iron your shirts treating HER like then?"

Not having a ready answer, Silver-tongue deflected her by going into accusation mode; "You are too erratic," he snarled; "I want things done in a more structured way!"

The sword was forgotten in the heat of her anger. Furious, she told him to get out and threw his stuff out after him. It was an anti-climax because his 'stuff' only amounted to a packet of tomato soup, which she watched bounce down the steps. He left, she smarted, the King sighed and the dragon smirked.

"Did you see what happened there?" he asked. "Don't give in to your anger. You know the response the dragon wants! You must give the opposite response," he counselled Joanna.

'Better a patient person than a warrior, one with self-control than one who takes a city,'" he taught her from Proverbs 16:32 (NIV).

"My patience has worn thin. I'm used to people believing their wants and needs are more important than mine, but he is in a league of his own. Who does he think he is? He has the biggest sense of entitlement I've ever seen," Joanna grumbled.

"You have to stop caring about his wants and needs," the King warned; "He doesn't appreciate it. You've tried all your life to earn approval, and he's not going to give it to you. He thinks he's deserving and special. All that will happen is he'll use you and expect even more."

The next time Silver-tongue verbally attacked her she said with an icy smile and ground teeth; "I know how you want me to react, but I'm not going to get upset this time – I'm handing this to the Lord. Oh, and another thing – I don't need your approval."

Silver-tongue looked surprised. He needed Joanna to look to him for approval, and only had one script for her to follow. Who was this changeling? He felt more and more control slip away.

The battle continued. Silver-tongue wasn't the only one who wounded her. When the dragon found Joanna resisting him, he tried an attack through another avenue; her mother - who conveniently for him had gone bi-polar. When elevated he'd change her from a happy, kind and sunny natured woman to someone who was really nasty and not safe to be around. Joanna and her sisters had a name for her demonic alter-ego; 'the Bull.'

As usual for when she was high, her 'mother' had been spreading gossip and slander about Joanna. The familiar pattern was to slander Joanna and then turn up afterwards with her yapping husband in tow to pester her.

Her eyes would glitter with mania as she fed off Joanna's anguish. It was a sick Jekyll and Hyde relationship Joanna didn't want.

Wishing she'd been allowed to stay in Sydney where she was safe, Joanna cursed her.

"Don't curse, the dragon feeds off cursing," the King warned.

"It's true though. She's not a mother," Joanna replied bitterly.

"I know. But she was bereft of her own mother," the Lord replied in the face of Joanna's rejection.

"That doesn't help me or my children. We all have to make choices. I don't want her," Joanna replied angrily.

Joanna's mother had been abandoned by her birth mother when she was about three. Joanna knew nothing about her maternal grandmother other than she'd been born in Geelong, Australia and she may have been adopted. If adopted, she was probably from a long line of ostrich mothers.

Now it was affecting the next generation. "You say bad words about us," Joanna's four-year old son accused her mother, and Joanna noticed he never went near his Nana for a cuddle.

"Can't you see what's happening? This has been going on for generations," Joanna cried to the King.

"I know, but you and your sisters are breaking the cycle that she can't," he replied. "You haven't abused or abandoned your own children, and you're shielding them as best as you can. The dragon wants to have her doubly rejected. Find the door the dragon is using to get at you - and close it."

"Is the door my anger?" she asked.

"Yes, and you have the right to be angry," the King answered; *"But take note of this: Everyone should be quick to listen, slow to speak and slow to become angry, for man's anger does not produce the righteousness that I desire." (James 1:19-20)*

How could she let it go? But Joanna found she could not hold onto both the sword and her anger. It made the sword too heavy. Choosing to keep the sword and drop her anger, the princess within spoke to her mother; "I've heard what you said about me. Why do you do it? I'm not going to get angry this time. I want to talk to you about your words!"

Her mother hung up.

The King smiled; "Now we wait …"

Later, the phone rang. It was her sisters, who were all agog; "Good God! What happened? What have you done to Mum? These are her words; "I've said bad things about Joanna, and I need to apologise."

"It's true! She is back in her own mind and wants to say sorry. No bull!"

They were all amazed. It was indeed a first. The word 'sorry' was not in their mother's vocabulary. She had never owned her behaviour or apologised before this, and she'd never snapped out of a high - ever. Manic episodes always lasted for months.

Joanna laughed and laughed.

"*Resist the devil and he will flee from you*," the King had said during sword practise.

The dragon had indeed fled. Good riddance!

He could not go back there to wound her. If he tried, the princess within would be waiting … and Joanna would now go for him rather than her mother. For the first time in her life, she felt like she had some control.

"*So then, submit yourselves to God. Resist the Devil, and he will run away from you. Come near to God, and he will come near to you.*" *James 4:7 (GNT)*

Chapter Three

Joanna smiled as she looked at the other pieces of armour the King had given her, a belt, breastplate, boots, shield, and helmet. They all shone with light. She felt like a warrior princess.

"So stand ready, with truth as a belt tight around your waist, with righteousness as your breastplate, and as your shoes the readiness to announce the good news of peace. At all times carry faith as a shield; for with it you will be able to put out all the burning arrows shot by the Evil One.
And accept salvation as a helmet, and the word of God as the sword which the Spirit gives you." Ephesians 6:14-17 (GNT)

The King bade Joanna to stop Silver-tongue from visiting. Silver-tongue readily yielded. It suited him, knowing there were a lot of family events to attend with his wife and family in the triangle where Joanna was not welcome. Joanna was always there to go back to when he had nothing better to do.

Silver-tongue wormed his way back in to her life weeks later. He arrived on April Fools' Day 1996 with a cardboard box full of clothes, saying he was 'moving in'.

Joanna looked up from the oven she was cleaning. It was news to her. "This is your last chance," she warned, shelving her doubts along with the oven tray.

Silver-tongue wasn't worried, she was lucky to have him.

"That which is crooked cannot be made straight: and that which is lacking cannot be numbered," the King warned, quoting a passage from Ecclesiastes.

Nothing much changed. A box of clothes underneath the bed joined the packet of soup in the pantry; and he now joined them at the table, staying most nights. Silver-tongue was still a creature of the night. On his days off he was either at his place where his wife lived, or he was out hunting. Joanna didn't like it. Alone during the day, she walked a lonely path through no man's land.

Joanna was coming to realise the 'relationship' had been sustained by false promises. Each time she tried to walk away, Silver-tongue made a promise so she'd stay. If she asked about the broken promises, he'd deflect her by launching a personal attack, turning the reason for the broken promises into some perceived deficiency or shortfall on her part.

She would then have to 'prove' herself before he'd 'commit' to the promise.

The personal attacks were vicious, but lately his poison darts had been bouncing off a shield she was carrying.

Helped by the King, Joanna was learning how to wield the shield of faith. The shield was high enough to protect her entire body and designed to stop the dragon's fiery darts.

Silver-tongue didn't like her shield. Wanting her to drop it, he tripped her up constantly. Sometimes the shield was too big for Joanna to carry.

From the way she was being treated it became obvious Silver-tongue did not have any faith in her; in fact, he thought the worst of her. She was made responsible for everything that was wrong in the 'relationship.' He'd also upped the barrage of verbal assaults.

Exhausted, Joanna dropped her shield, asking the King for help as she couldn't go on. The way was too hard.

Knowing she was too worn down to lift the shield of faith, he asked her to carry it, saying "Courage is the conquering of fear by faith. If you don't fight then I can't guide you to freedom. You'll continue to walk the right way on the wrong path, and you'll never know any peace.

The dragon will continue to fight for what is yours. Do you want this?"

Taking the shield, Joanna the warrior princess wearily asked "Lord is it not the prince who is supposed to wear armour and kill dragons?"

"Only in fairy tales" he replied smiling.

The King got Joanna to examine the shield more closely.

"This shield has substance," he explained; *'Now faith is the substance of things hoped for, the evidence of things not seen.' Hebrews 11:1 (KJV)*

"You have used the shield already – last year, when you warded off that attack in the Pits," he reminded her.

"Yes, I remember all the fiery darts bouncing off me," she smiled.

"I doubt the dragon will forget it either," the King laughed.

The victory in the Pits

Picking up her shield, Joanna thought back to the events of 1994, the year before. Emotionally drained by the counselling, the death of her father and the abusive relationship; she had nothing left in the tank.

Silver-tongue wanted constant attention, which she was too distressed to give him. He didn't care how he got it – if not by charm, then he'd get it by wounding; and he would not let her be.

He ignored her pleas to be left alone and would not hand his key back. She'd given him a key before he'd turned nasty, a mistake she did not repeat at her new place. He was letting himself into her house even though he'd been told to stay away. He was like a venomous snake, full of spite, lashing out because he couldn't make her bereavement all about him.

To add to her misery, Silver-tongue convinced the counsellor she wasn't dealing with her grief. The counsellor didn't know and couldn't see he was adding to her grief. Joanna wasn't being given the space to grieve for her father as she needed to. There was no one to lean on or turn to. She didn't know she could get a protection order - it was something the counsellor did not tell her.

It seemed she was in a dark forest where she couldn't see the wood for the trees. How could she function? She had been fighting the dragon in her own strength and was near exhaustion.

The only thing that kept her going was the vow she'd made never to abandon her children. One night the King watched as she tucked her young son into bed. He heard her say "Son, you don't need to pretend you're sick if you're worried about attending a birthday party by yourself. Mummy can't help you if you don't tell her."

"You need to take your own advice," he said as she came downstairs.

"What do you mean?" she asked.

"Your thoughts are killing you. I can see it all churning through your mind - the anger, the hurt and the injustice. It's like watching death by a thousand cuts," he replied with concern, adding; "I can't help you if you don't tell me. You must give me those thoughts."

She frowned as she replied "I can't – my thoughts are foul and accompanied by a lot of wrath, resentment and swear words. He speaks with a forked tongue and spits venom. It goes into my mind.

"Don't worry, I can handle the foulness and swearwords," he replied, adding, "Tomorrow, we start."

The bad thoughts started the next morning, when Joanna woke up and walked down the stairs to put the kettle on in the small kitchen. As soon as she started to entertain the first thought, the Lord cut in, prompting her to give it to him.

Silently she handed the thought over; "Lord, I give this to you."

The thoughts kept on coming. Joanna held her ground, silently handing the thoughts over.

Alone with her children, she prayed all that day and the next; keeping at it silently, doggedly and stubbornly. The hate gained no purchase or traction in her mind. The dragon was getting frustrated, because he couldn't get at her. She was guarding herself with a shield which grew stronger each time she deflected a bad thought. The more he attacked, the bigger it grew.

The King took the captives she handed him, waiting for the big one.

After two days of handing the Lord all the hate and all the hurt, Joanna encountered him in a dream. She found herself on the ground floor of a house with a flat roof. Hearing him call her name, she followed his voice upstairs, walking into a room that was completely white. It seemed to be a bathroom, but there was no sink or bath - just the King with a sack.

She stood before him waiting. He looked comforting, but his words weren't.

"There is a snake in your pocket," he told her as he held the sack open. Even though there were no snakes in her country, she believed him.

"What? Take it from me!" she cried, springing back alarmed and surprised.

He shook his head; "No. You know what to do. Give it to me."

"But it will bite!" she said, frightened.

"You won't be harmed," he said reassuringly.

Digging into her pocket Joanna retrieved a small death adder, which immediately sank its fangs into her hand.

"Lord, I give this to you!" she said with a shudder, shaking it off into the sack.

Quickly coiling the neck of the sack closed, the King said "Well done daughter, your faith has made you well. It's time to wake now."

Joanna awoke to find two gifts the King had left for her. The first gift was a song, which was playing on the radio. Rubbing her eyes bemusedly, she looked at her clock radio. It was strange because she always had it set on alarm. The alarm slider had been moved, all by itself.

The song playing was "I can see clearly now" by Johnny Nash. The words of the song were laden with meaning and promise. She'd come out of the woods.

"Look all around, there's nothing but blue sky," she heard the music play.

"All of the bad feelings had disappeared," she marvelled, experiencing the peace of God that went beyond all understanding. The emotional pain was gone.

The second gift was a healing. She'd endured a hacking cough for the last ten months; ever since that week of unbearable stress where she'd been hit by the three things at once - her father's cancer diagnosis, her bird's death, and Silver-tongue's 'plan B' betrayal. The cough had come with the shock and had been as hard to shake off as Silver-tongue.

Happy, Joanna went to the Doctor with a big smile on her face saying "We can cancel the chest X-ray." The doctor was surprised the cough, which had resisted two lots of antibiotics, had gone. "Jesus healed me" she told him. Impressed, the doctor told her that Jesus did indeed heal patients, but they did not admit it or speak about it openly.

It was after her healing that Silver-tongue turned up with the Riddler, the new counsellor, begging her to give him another chance.

The Breastplate of Righteousness

"I expected you to be here earlier," Joanna said, hurt, disappointed and let down yet again. Silver-tongue felt pleased, empowered that he'd hurt her.
He employed various means with which to control Joanna, and one of them was through refusal.
"You have no reason to expect anything of me," he said, quoting the Gestalt prayer by Frederick S Perls; "*I do my thing and you do yours. I am not in this world to live up to your expectations, and you are not in this world to live up to mine. You are you and I am I, and if by chance we find each other, then it's beautiful.*"
Pleased with his silvery recitation of the poem he smiled, but Joanna saw right through him. It was a stupid poem and it disgusted her.
The princess rose up, and looking at him with disdain she replied, "*Yes and a fool can use a proverb about as well as a cripple can use his legs.*" (Proverbs 26:7)
Silver-Tongue glared at the princess.
Silver-tongue's refusal led to resentment and Joanna's anger grew. She had lived for his approval and wanted to make him happy, but that was gradually changing, for her eyes were now upon the King.

"You are trying to walk the right way up a crooked path," the King warned Joanna. Joanna felt haggard and deathly tired. They surveyed the ground she had gained from the dragon. It was devastated and barren. Nothing had been able to grow there.
The King asked her to look at him. She met his eyes, eyes that contained the wisdom of ages. In his presence she could feel his power and authority.
He said, "I know you are tired of fighting, but you have to go back into battle again."
The warrior princess was weary. "I'm tired. I have no strength left for sword or shield. The dragon was your enemy long before I came here. He only hates me because I'm yours. You go kill it, Lord."

"You must fight," he replied; "This is your life. You have to make a stand, or you will never know any peace."
 The next day she prepared for battle. "Lord, I cannot see you, where are you?" she cried out, trying to shoulder into her breastplate. It was too heavy and tight to put on.
At last, the Lord appeared. "I cannot help you. You need to put your armour on first."
"I know that, Lord, and I am trying!" she sobbed. "Why does it not fit?" she asked in despair; "I haven't put any weight on."
"Just the weight of the world!" the King remarked adding; "The breastplate of righteousness cannot fit over resentment. You can only wear one or the other."
"Then help me get the resentment off," she begged.
"No, I cannot, for it will only go right back on. You need to deal with the cause of the resentment. You have to deal with the man you call Silver-tongue," he replied.
Joanna could hear the dragon's laughter, knowing how she'd be ignored, or attacked.
Her eyes narrowed as she remembered her crook. Suddenly the abused and down trodden woman disappeared, replaced by the princess;
"What is that in my cottage by the fireplace, you dragon scum? Who gave me that! Don't you know that the King gifted that to me with his words and his promise that his house will be my home for as long as I live!
Do you know the authority I have over you in the King's name? I'm a daughter of the King, and I know that he hears me, you liar. I know my birthright, and I will not be cheated out of it!"

Afraid she was going to start quoting scripture, the dragon backed off. Joanna was resisting him and getting harder to control as the princess within gained strength.

Left in peace, Joanna smiled up at the King through her tears. "Lord, I can live with you, but not with Silver-tongue. I no longer trust him, and I'm afraid of his words," she said, adding; *'My companion attacks his friends; he violates his covenant. His speech is smooth as butter, yet war is in his heart; his words are more soothing than oil, yet they are drawn swords.' Psalm 55:20-21* (NIV)

She asked; "How can I deal with my resentment and show him his fault, when he thinks he is perfect?"
"Don't run ahead," the Lord replied; "I will use your relationship with Silver-tongue because he draws out your enemies. You can learn from this."

Joanna turned to walk away. "Where are you going?" he asked. "To the land between the rock and the hard place," she replied bitterly; "The resentment is getting too much to bear. It's grown even worse with Silver-tongue, for it seems he does not care about me.
'When I look beside me, I see that there is no one to help me, No one to protect me, no one cares for me.'" Psalm 142:4 (GNT)

The King didn't want her to walk off in self-pity.
"Forgive me," she asked, looking back at him; "I want your righteousness. It's so much better than that ill-fitting, chafing resentment. I know that you will not lift it off, but neither will Silver-tongue. He *wants* me to wear it! I don't know how to get if off. I've worn it all my life."

"Why do you head for this hard place where you know you will find no comfort, when all you have to do is seek my advice?" the King asked.
Joanna replied "Lord, don't you see? I have no right to ask you for help. I have no right to seek you in this matter between Silver-tongue and I."
The King asked "Who determined this right?"
Joanna paused.
"Uncertainty did, Lord," she finally answered.
The King lifted her chin and looked at her; "Remember what my servant Eve said? You must come to me with certainty."
She nodded and bowed at the King's feet.

Joanna eyed the breastplate.
"How can I get righteousness, when I am not righteous?" she asked.

"No one is righteous. All have sinned and fallen short of my law" the King replied, offering her redemption; "You are in right standing before my Father not from keeping the law, but through faith in me; and this righteousness comes by faith."

At his words the princess within Joanna rose up. As he helped her shoulder into the breastplate of righteousness he promised, *"I will lead you along the path of righteousness, even for my own name's sake."* Psalm 23:3

The King wanted Joanna to go on the offensive.
"I am not happy about you giving in to the demands of this man you call Silver-Tongue. Now turn around and ask for what *you want* instead," he said.

Joanna was afraid. She had been punished for wanting things.
"Lord, I don't know how to ask for what I want," she replied; "It's even worse with Silver-tongue - because he *promised me* he cared. I used to wait for what I wanted, and then I'd prompt him with clues, and wait again. My needs would be ignored.
When I finally asked, in beggar's clothes and resentment, Silver-tongue would say 'I hadn't asked in the prescribed manner.' Now I'm afraid of the refusal. It's hurtful."
"He has found so many ways to refuse me; she continued tiredly; 'I used the wrong language', or 'it was a demand.' I've stopped asking, and have ended up expecting nothing for myself. In so doing, my trust and hope have died. Yet his demands are constant and he expects to get what he wants."

"You must overcome your fear of refusal," the King replied, adding "Love is not ill-mannered or selfish. If he refuses after you have asked, you will be left in no doubt about what kind of man he is."

The warning

Joanna stopped giving in to Silver-Tongue's demands, even making some of her own. Silver-tongue noticed. He watched her growing relationship with the Lord with calculating eyes.

He got religion the year before, after Joanna had stopped seeing him, telling him she wanted a man who was after the King's heart. Joanna had tried to give him the benefit of the doubt when he turned up at her door with a Bible.

Silver-tongue spent time studying the Bible to see if it contained anything that was of use and seized upon the passage about women submitting to their husbands. He quoted it to her, referring to himself as "her husband."

He cherry picked the verses, ignoring the first verse that said *"Submit yourselves to one another because of your reverence for Christ." Ephesians 5:21 (GNT)*

"You're not my husband" Joanna said derisively, hating his handling of the King's word and yet torn between reality and hope. What if his professed faith in the King proved to be genuine? If it was, he would change.

Confused, she wondered whether Silver-Tongue really had become a Christian – but he must have been serious as he'd gone as far as to be baptised. "Who would do that?" she thought. She did not want to discourage a new believer.

It didn't occur to her that he'd become a "believer" in order to use the Bible to control her.

She took the matter to the Lord; "Silver-tongue said he has met you at a group of believers and he received the great gift of your spirit, for he can now pray in tongues."

The King glowered; "*A man named Simon the Sorcerer once approached my apostles wanting to buy the power I gave them. He was told my gift cannot be bought with money; and to repent of his wickedness.*" (Acts 8:18-23)

"*What good will it be for a man if he gains the whole world, yet forfeits his soul?*" he asked; "*Or what can a man give in exchange for his soul?*" Matthew 16:26 (NIV)

"My words are not to be used for personal gain, or to gain power over others. That's called witchcraft." He added; "I am going to question you about him, and I want you to think about your answers."

"Is he patient, is he kind?"

"No," Joanna answered.

"Does he envy?"

"He tries to hide it, but yes, he's envious."

"Is he boastful, or proud?"

She nodded.

"Does he honour you?"

"No," she answered sadly.

"Is he self-seeking?"

"Very," she answered.

"Is he easily angered, and does he keep a record of wrongs?"

"Yes, especially when he doesn't get his own way," she answered.

"Does he delight in evil?"

"Yes," Joanna had to answer.

"Does he rejoice with the truth?"

"No - anything but," she replied.

"Does he protect you, trust you, hope in you, and persevere with you?"

"No," Joanna replied flatly.

Closing the chapter of 1 Corinthians 13, the King replied; *"If I speak in the tongues of men and of angels, but have not love, I am only a resounding gong or a clanging cymbal."*

Torn between despair at the King's words and hope in Silver-tongue's promises, Joanna hesitated.

"He could change," she promised herself, clinging to hope. She needed to see if Silver-tongue was real about being a follower of the King. If he was the Lord would bring him to repentance and make him a better man. Then he'd learn how to love.

There was a proverb that said *'if the dross was removed from the silver, a silversmith can produce a vessel.' (Proverbs 25:4).*

If only it were so. Deciding to give him another chance, she ignored her feelings until the day her body spoke for her.

She was working when Silver-tongue ran his hands down her back. Her whole body shuddered in revulsion as she jerked away from his touch. The unconscious action spoke volumes.

Joanna knew he'd noticed. No words were said.

The Lord waited, wanting her to trust her feelings.

One night she had a vivid, unsettling dream. A lynx cat had a lamb by its throat on a bank of white snow. The lamb's blood had spilled onto the snow, staining it red. The lynx cat did not relinquish its hold on the lamb. It watched her with the eyes of a predator.

Joanna felt a strong sense of warning.

What was the King saying?

For God does speak—now one way, now another, though no one perceives it. In a dream, in a vision of the night, when deep sleep falls on people as they slumber in their beds, he may speak in their ears and terrify them with warnings, to turn them from wrongdoing and keep them from pride, to preserve them from the pit, their lives from crossing the river. Job 33:14-18 (NIV)

The promise

Joanna was approaching a milestone. Her daughter was about to start school, giving her more freedom, and she had to buy a house or her benefit would stop. She needed the benefit. It was too soon to return to full time work, and she could not live on her part time wages.

It was time to make a decision. She'd been on her own for three years now, waiting for Silver-tongue. If she had to buy a house by herself, she would be walking away from him for good.

Silver-tongue seemed not to care about her change of circumstances. He joined her briefly and unwillingly at her daughter's fifth birthday party, before going his own way, hunting deer for the weekend.

She remembered a promise the King had given her in his Word. It was an awesome promise, too difficult to believe; *'You will be called by a new name, a name given by the Lord himself. You will be like a beautiful crown for the Lord. No longer will you be called "forsaken," or your land be called "the deserted wife."*

Your new name will be "God is pleased with her." Your land will be called "happily married," because the Lord is pleased with you.' Isaiah 62:2-4 (GNT)

"Will I really be married?" Joanna asked the Lord, conflicted about his promise;
"Yes" the Lord replied.

"Happily?" she asked.

"Yes" he replied.

"But why would you give me a second chance, when you say in Malachi 2:16 that you hate divorce?" she asked, thinking of the broken vows from her first marriage.

The King spoke;

'Do not be afraid—you will not be disgraced again; you will not be humiliated.
You will forget your unfaithfulness as a young wife, and your desperate loneliness as a widow.
Your Creator will be like a husband to you— the LORD *Almighty is his name.*
The holy God of Israel will save you— he is the ruler of all the world.
You are like a young wife, deserted by her husband and deeply distressed.
But the LORD *calls you back to him and says: "For one brief moment I left you;*
with deep love I will take you back.
I turned away angry for only a moment,
but I will show you my love forever." So says the LORD *who saves you.'*
Isaiah 54:4-8 (GNT)

Comforted, Joanna tried to get her head around the King's promise. It was almost too good to be true.

"Who will I marry?"

"Someone I have *chosen*," replied the King.

"Do I not have a choice?" she asked.

"Yes, you have freewill," he answered, "But I remind you are now one of MINE. You gave your life to me; and I am the Lord. Let me rule. My choice for you is better; my will for your life is perfect. Learn to trust," he replied.

He did not ask "And your choices have got you where?"

The King knew Joanna would need closure with Silver-tongue, but he wanted her to have the promise of a happy marriage to bring her hope. She needed hope.

The decision

Joanna walked alone through 'No man's land,' a miserable grey area she'd ended up in because of Silver-tongue's murky marital status.

"How many times can I tell you I'm not married?" Silver-tongue would ask, looking aggrieved when Joanna asked about his wife or property. Joanna badly needed him to move on - to either reconcile or get divorced. Was he still with his wife, or not? Until he did move on, Joanna was left stranded in limbo, with no place in his life. Worse than that, what was her status?

When they talked about his family Silver-tongue tried to get away with; "It's not them that's important, it's us," but it led to Joanna getting really angry.

"This is *not* my idea of a commitment," she remarked, frustrated, hurt and disappointed.

"I've talked to the experts, and they all agree you're not ready for that," Silver-tongue answered smoothly, negating her for the last time.

Left speechless, Joanna spent the day planning how to take the control away from him.

At the end of the day, she handed him his box of clothes. "This isn't working out," she said ushering him down the steps; "I need you to go back to your parent's place and sort yourself out, while *I* figure out just what it is that I *am* ready for!"

The whole thing had become about him. How had she got to this?

Silver-tongue had constructed a triangle where he ate with his wife, slept at his parents, and visited her. Joanna had been putting up with it for two years. Wondering how she'd been manipulated into accepting 'the triangle,' her mind went back to early 1994.

"My children need me ..." he'd begun after 'plan B' had gone awry and he'd moved in with his parents. "I'd like to eat meals with them. Will that be okay?" he'd asked disingenuously.

"Of course," Joanna answered, wanting to support him. She didn't realise he was constructing a triangle in the land of limbo.

The princess within appeared. "Please lead me out of 'No man's land'" she asked, bowing before the Lord. "I deserve so much more than this."

"Yes, it's time to come off the crooked path," the King said, leading her by the hand.

Conflicted, Joanna looked back. Couldn't the Lord make the path straight? Tugging on his hand, she made a final appeal for him to set things right. Joanna believed love had to be earned. If only Silver-tongue could *see* she'd earned the love and approval he'd withheld from her.

"Please, Lord, can't you make him see?" she begged; "Although Silver-tongue can't accept me the way I am now, I know he would if he resolved things and we got together. I know at times I've been moody and unhappy. I have lost so much these last three years and I'm stressed out because he's procrastinated. He told me that his commitment to me is irrevocable and forever; and that he *is* on his own – that's why I was still trying to make it work."

The King listened to her in silence as he watched Joanna go into the last stage of grief; acceptance.

She sighed; "I can't understand it. At first, he was so tender, so charming. He put me first and he really cared about me. I wanted that back *so* badly. Can't you change the way he regards me?" she pleaded sadly.

"No, you need to change the way you regard *him*," the King responded; "*Why should you be beaten anymore? Why do you persist in rebellion? Your whole head is injured, your whole heart afflicted.*" Isaiah 1:5-6 (NIV)

He gazed into her heart and found the princess. Joanna was strong enough now to hear the cold hard facts, and he spelled them out for her;

"Listen, this man preys on vulnerable women. He had done it before, many times. He's a master at manipulation and control. He doesn't care about you or believe in you. As far as he's concerned, you're not worthy of him or marriage, despite all his talk of 'commitment.'"

"He said he loved me," Joanna cried. "Why did he persist with me, if that was his belief?"

"It suited him to regard you that way. There's only room for him in that heart. He wants to control you *and* keep his wife," replied the King with compassion.

"That is not love. It was never love, was it? You had to stand back and let me learn that for myself!" she cried in pain. She had invested everything into this relationship; and now she was left with nothing but the broken pieces of a shattered life.

"What is going to happen to me now, Lord?" she asked at last, feeling numb.

The King replied, bringing her hope; "Without him, your life is going to get better, trust me. I will find you the right man."

"Delight yourself in me, and I will give you your heart's desire." *(Psalm 37:4)*

"I believe in you, and I choose to be free," Joanna said, walking off the crooked path. She was trying to be brave but a river of tears ran down her face.

After he'd comforted her the King led Joanna into the Kingdom. She followed him through an archway in the castle wall. Autumn leaves fell around them making a red and golden carpet on the ground in the blue-grey light.

As they kicked their way through the leaves the path of righteousness opened up before them.

The King said; "This is the path that leads to life. It's also called 'the everlasting way'. Along this path is immortality. It will be dark at first, but the path of the righteous is like the morning sun, shining ever brighter till the full light of day. At times you will slip, but if you trust me, I will guide you in the way of wisdom.

'Wisdom will save you from the ways of wicked men, from men whose words are perverse, who have left the straight paths to walk in dark ways, who delight in doing wrong and rejoice in the perverseness of evil, whose paths are crooked and who are devious in their ways.'" Proverbs 2:12-15 (NIV)

Picking up her lamp, she smiled at the King and started following him on the long journey towards the brightening horizon. It was the dawn of a new day. As they walked, she remembered a proverb from her earthly father; "The darkest hour is before dawn."

The first wish

Joanna bought a house without telling Silver-tongue. Built in 1910, it had a lot of character with leadlight windows, pressed-tin ceilings and a big backyard. More importantly, it was in a good neighbourhood for her children to grow up in. She packed in a quiet and surreptitious manner so that Silver-tongue wouldn't notice anything amiss when he came to visit.

More than once she'd tried to break free, but Silver-tongue's hold had been too strong. This time it was different. By buying her own house, she was taking control of her future, and she would build a new life without him.

The Lord gave her a gift after she bought the house. Leading her into the Kingdom, he showed her an acorn, the first seed to be planted on the ground made barren. It was not tangible but she could see it. "You will know when it's time to sow" he promised.

One evening in late autumn when the wind blew cold outside her cottage, the King joined Joanna in front of the fire she'd lit.

Looking at him, she said, "This is the season when the wind grows cold and the land sleeps. In this time, I will follow you and practise what you've taught me. With your help, I will rebuild my life. Please restore my soul."

"I will," he replied, "and if you seek first my Kingdom, I will fulfil the promises I made. I replant, rebuild and restore. I will not fail to do what I have promised."

"Lord, I'm strong enough now to break away. I know you have forgiven my involvement with Silver-tongue and I know I'll not walk alone. You have taught me well, and this time I'll do it, but please stand by me" she asked, looking to him for reassurance.

"You know I'll be there beside you," the King promised.

"What is going to happen to me after I have gained my freedom?" she asked dubiously, worrying about the future. All she could see ahead was a desert of loneliness.

The King looked at her as she added a log to the fire; "You have a long road ahead. Who you travel with depends on faith; faith in me, faith in yourself and faith in your fellow man."

"I have difficulty believing in myself after being belittled and undermined by Silver-tongue" she confessed.

"Whose eyes will you see yourself in – mine or his?" he challenged her.

"I am sorry, Lord," Joanna replied, "I want to see myself through your eyes. What made me choose this man in the first place?"

"He chose you," the King replied, "You fell for his words and his outwards appearance. Looks, intellect, wealth, a glib tongue and a white charger are not everything. Learn to look at the heart of a man. See a man through my eyes.

'Pay no attention to how tall and handsome he is. I have rejected him, because I do not judge as man judges. Man looks at the outward appearance, but I look at the heart.'" 1 Samuel 6:7 (GNT)

"You're right. Please bring me a man who is the exact opposite of Silver-tongue" Joanna asked recklessly, on a wish and not a prayer.

Cocking an eyebrow, the King looked at her as if to ask "Am I the Fairy Godmother?"

The Minstrel

Joanna knew Silver-tongue wanted lots of freedom - and gave it to him. While he was off doing his own thing he would not notice she was packing. In the winter of the year 1996 she broke off the relationship with Silver-tongue completely. As expected, Silver-tongue did not believe the "relationship" was over.

At first indifferent and cold about her decision, Silver-tongue believed he would win her back with his customary words and false promises. Previous attempts at ridding herself of him had failed. She had still loved him and taken him back on the basis of his promises; none of which had been kept.

This time her decision had been final. Joanna implemented the plan she'd devised; a slow withdrawal culminating in a complete break.

A few weeks after telling Silver-tongue it was over she made a new friend. Her first impression of him was not good as he strolled past her in the school corridor. All she could see was a trashy guy wearing overalls unzipped to his navel.

He had a hard look about him that she didn't like. She watched him go outside and strut amongst the school mothers like a cocky little bantam rooster in a hen house.

Unfortunately, their children bonded and quickly became close friends, which brought them together like magnets. He invited her in when she collected her children from an after-school visit.

Joanna always met the parents so she visited with him.
She was surprised to find he was friendly and likeable, although he told her that he did not like the King, or the King's subjects.

Joanna met the King's watchful eyes. "Well, my first impressions were wrong. You were right to tell me not to judge by outwards appearances" she remarked, adding "He's in for a surprise when he learns who I obey."

"When he learns who you *sometimes* obey," chided the King.

She found out he was the father of two adorable little blonde girls who he was bringing up alone; and they'd recently moved into the area. The girl's mother had died of a heroin overdose in Sydney.

They became friends, which suited Joanna. His friendship was a salve to her wounded heart - and even better, he offered to help her move. She introduced him to the King.

Joanna dubbed her new friend Douglas 'the Minstrel' from playing the guitar. She was pleased to see him sit at Silver-tongue's place at the table when they came around one evening for dinner.

He had a wicked sense of humour which was refreshing after Silver-tongue's heavy and humourless presence. Laughter came back into the house.

One afternoon, Silver-tongue came around thinking she had picked his assignment up from the college where they both studied part time. He was surprised to find that she had not concerned herself with it. It was out of character for her to not cover for him in his absence. After all, she was his study partner.

"We're over. Find someone else to copy your work off!" she told him, looking at him with dislike.

He ignored her. She was just being moody again.

His eyes narrowed as he saw the huge pile of wood that had been chopped and neatly stacked against the house. He'd only chopped wood for her once - for show when her ex-husband had come over from Australia to visit the children.

He knew she chopped wood every day after school, a chore that took up time. Who'd chopped all this wood?

He was afraid to ask, knowing he'd be shown up for not lifting a finger to help. She knew what he was thinking and stifled a grin. It was nearly three o'clock. "Aren't you getting the children from school?" he asked.

"No, Douglas is," she answered, with a mocking smile.

He did not like her answer. "Who is Douglas?" he demanded.

"He's not someone you need to concern yourself with," she answered, looking at him coldly; "I told you a month ago it was over between us. *I meant it.* Now go away."

Silver-tongue couldn't bear to think HE would be the reason she would walk away. He needed to believe he was perfect and God-given.
The fact that she would remove him from her life was an assault on his ego. Blaming Douglas for Joanna's loss of interest, he would not accept that it was over and demanded she stop seeing Douglas.

With a look of disgust, she told him again to go away and stop bothering her. Silver-tongue stalked both her and Douglas from the shadows.

The King sent her best friend Nerida and husband to help her move, as well as Douglas (the Minstrel) and her father-outlaw. Silver-tongue searched for Joanna after he was sure Nerida, who he regarded with fear and loathing, had gone.

When he found her new house he quickly found he was not welcome, but he hung on with one grasping tentacle after the other. It reminded Joanna of the scene in the movie Alien, where Ripley had to blast the monster from the airlock. It took weeks to finally get rid of him.

In the days that followed she cried when she found herself alone. Her hard-won freedom felt like an empty void.

The Minstrel's friendship helped her across the first part of the void, but it also caused her to stumble. It gave her someone new to think about besides Silver-tongue, but it confused her as well. She'd had a date with him, but didn't let it go any further.

The Minstrel was indeed the exact opposite of Silver-tongue, but not in a good way. He was a blonde bogan - an uncultured person with no wealth and an ancient car called 'Noddy.' It seemed the King had indeed granted her wish. Was this the man he'd promised?

"My father prayed for a Christian wife for me" the Minstrel had told her, as he thanked the King for their friendship.

The Minstrel's parents were divorced and his father sounded like a very forceful man.

Joanna was doubtful about being the answer to his father's prayers.

"I'm not ready for another relationship yet" she told him, knowing the King would not want her to go rushing into anything at this stage.

Wisdom was needed. While the father had sought the Lord for a Christian daughter-in-law, he had not prayed for his son to come to know the Lord. Nor did he seek first the Kingdom of God.

The Minstrel sheltered behind his father's words, but when she did not fall into his bed, he told her he wanted to pursue other women as well. Seeing he could not be trusted, Joanna backed away.

It did not take them long to fall out with each other.

"I'm not your type," the Minstrel said, speaking the truth. Although they had lived in Sydney and their children were inseparable, it was not enough.

His mind changed like the weather and he blew hot and cold. With his mercurial temperament it was difficult for her to gauge what his mood was going to be.

She'd had enough of mind games with Silver-tongue. She did not want or need a double minded man.

The King gave her a word of encouragement and warning; *"Consider it pure joy, whenever you face trials of many kinds, because you know that the testing of your faith produces perseverance. Let perseverance finish its work so that you may be mature and complete, not lacking anything.*

If you lack wisdom, you should ask me, for I the Lord give generously to all without finding fault, and it will be given to you.

But when you ask, you must believe and not doubt, because the one who doubts is like a wave of the sea, blown and tossed by the wind. That person should not expect to receive anything from me. Such a person is double-minded and unstable in all they do."
James 1:2-8 (NIV)

Kate and the crocodile

The King watched Joanna sleep. She'd granted herself a Saturday morning lie in while her ex-husband visited the children. He sighed. It was a rest which was soon to be interrupted. He needed to prepare her for the rudest awakening of her life.

In a dream, Joanna suddenly found herself in a desert in Egypt, overlooking a canal. A large crocodile threshed about in the water with a woman in its jaws. The woman reached out to her for help. Joanna moved as close to the edge of the canal as she could, but could not deal with the crocodile. "I can't reach you," she called out to the woman; "You have to break free!"

"I can't!" the woman screamed.

The dream rolled forward into real life as she awoke to a woman standing in her room! She was an old acquaintance from school days that Joanna caught up with from time to time.

Jolted to wakefulness, Joanna sat up and rubbed her eyes with a feeling of annoyance and regret. All she had wanted to do was sleep, but Thomas, her ex, had let her into the house.

Joanna had a nasty feeling about the dream.

"Why are you here?" she asked, thinking about the woman and the crocodile.

"I need to talk to you about Hugh (Silver-tongue)," the woman pleaded.

Ah, now she knew who the crocodile was. Joanna groaned as her feet hit the floor.

"What do you want from me?" she asked.

The woman chattered away as Joanna threw on a pair of jeans and headed for the kitchen where she made the coffee, her movements automatic.

"My relationship with Hugh started six weeks ago …" she began nervously.

Joanna's back stiffened. Turning around she asked, "So why did you wait *six weeks* to come to me?"

"He told me you were mentally ill and it would push you over the edge!" she replied.

Joanna felt sick. So, he was a slanderer as well. A taste of bile mingled with the coffee. Would her punishment never end? Six weeks before, she thought she'd finally gotten rid of him. Now he was back, sleeping with a friend and slandering her.

Shaken by the dream, Joanna knew she had to help. She did her best, painfully telling the truth about her affair. In her bruised mind, she no longer thought of what she grieved over as a 'relationship'.

As soon as Silver-tongue's new mistress 'Kate' had gone, Joanna left her children with their father, packed and got into her car, numbly driving north to Auckland.

Although she badly needed to distance herself from the on-going mess that was Silver-tongue, she knew it was a distance the days and the kilometres could not give her – unless she left everything and never went back. It wasn't an option, for she would never leave her children. At best this would give her a brief respite, until the children's father returned to Australia, and she'd have to return. All she wanted was to be left alone.

Kate contacted her upon her return, "I've listened to your counsel, and to what Hugh said in reply. There are so many things that conflict, and I need to know what's true. I've decided to remain with Hugh. Perhaps it will be different with me."

Again, she'd not been heard or believed! Joanna gave up and drank to the dregs the cup of bitterness.

"Why did you come to me if you did not want to listen?" she asked in anguish.

Kate had no answer.
"If you stay with him, you'll be sorry!" she ground out.
Kate was silent.

"What's he doing about his wife?" Joanna asked angrily.

"He did not say" Kate replied.

"Of course he didn't," Joanna retorted; "Does that not concern you? It should! He promised me the *world,* persuading me to leave *everything* - and all I got was the runaround, a life with no status, and endless strings of empty promises!"

"But he said he's going to make a commitment to me," Kate replied. She thought she knew why he couldn't make a commitment to Joanna.

Joanna choked; "Oh, really? Yeah, good luck with that. He said the same thing to me, but the only '*commitment*' I ever got from him was as his mistress. What will he now make you?"

"He's not after a mistress," Kate replied; "He wouldn't do that. He said he's a Christian."

Joanna snorted; "No he's not! That's another lie. He stopped going to church the minute he got baptised."
Shaking her head Kate replied "I know you're bitter, but I'll give it a chance."

Raking her hands through her dark hair in distress, Joanna's reply was terse; "Good luck. Stay with him if that's your choice, and suffer the consequences. I don't want anything more to do with you while you're with *him*. I need to heal! I can't go on hearing about him, or his lies."

The dragon appeared, laughing and sneering; "Be honest. You cannot bear the thought of those two together, can you?
And I am here to remind you. It did not take him long to replace you, did it?

You're not even worth grieving over! Perhaps she'll be better suited for him and succeed where you didn't. Perhaps she'll be accepted, where you never would have been.

Think of how she said he was very, very attracted to her, and he wanted to make a *commitment* to her."

Joanna tried to break free and run away. There was nowhere to go except the chill greyness - and even on the way to that place the dragon ran after her, laughing all the way. This time he intended to finish her off. He caught up with her; "Perhaps he'll really try this time and it will work between them. Think of all those new fresh feelings he has, while here you are buried in your grief."

The dragon laughed with delight as Joanna stumbled along sobbing, in a world of hurt.

It was too much for her to bear. Alone, she went into the land of chill grayness where there was nothing. The King sent a friend named White Flower to find her. Joanna didn't want company.

He who promised never to break the bruised twig or drown the tender reed, stood off at a distance to allow this test.

"Make it go away!" Joanna cried out in agony.

"I can't. There's no easy way through this" the King replied compassionately, adding "I know your pain. Did you think the dragon would just let you walk away, and not go after you?

He is a liar and the father of lies, the accuser who always fights in a dirty and underhand manner.

You belong to me so there will be no truces. He has come to steal, kill, and destroy. I have come that you may have life, and have it more abundantly."

"Have *what* more abundantly?" Joanna asked, sobbing and hiccupping; "Trouble? And grief?"

The King comforted her, asking "What happened to your armour and the friend I sent to help?"

"My armour?" Joanna replied wearily; "Are you serious? I did not stop to put it on before I ran - and now I'm too wounded. As for the friend; why should White Flower care? This is not her burden."

"Give her a chance," the King said; "You need someone to stand with you, someone who knows me and understands what an attack is."

White Flower lived only a few doors away and Joanna had known her for a while. She seemed to be a calm and gentle person, with a wicked sense of humour.

Joanna had been brought up to keep her pain to herself.

"*A broken spirit, who can bear?*" she asked herself from Proverbs 18:14.

Standing in the gap

White Flower gladly came to the aid of Joanna and joined in the fray. The dragon retreated, surprised that there were now two armour clad Princesses waiting for him, ready to go on the offensive.

Afterwards Joanna found herself beside a deep, clear pool of water. It was a quiet, still place where the silence waited for prayers. The Lord was there. *"Be still, and know that I am God"* she heard. The water reflected in his eyes as he looked at her, saying "I need you to pray for Kate."

Looking away, Joanna replied "She has chosen her path. We both know where it will end - in the desert of need, next to the ocean of pain, where the waves of hurt roll in. I can't stop her going there. Let others pray for her. She knows lots of people."

"Yes, others can pray for her, but I need an intercessor – someone who will stand in the gap and pray, standing in her shoes" the King replied.

Joanna understood. "I can see why you want me for the job" she replied, sighing; "I'll do it, even though I don't want to."

"Tears may flow in the night, but joy will come in the morning," he promised.

One day Kate appeared, looking fragile. Her smile was brittle. "I have come to tell you that it is over. I have broken free. The King gave me the strength to break it off."

"Thank God!" Joanna replied with heartfelt relief.
To celebrate, they ate together. Over dinner Kate said "I've met some bad men, but this one was an emotional psychopath."

"Yes, he's got no conscience," Joanna agreed. "I read the book you recommended, 'Men who hate women and the women who love them' and it nailed him. He has all the characteristics of a narcissist - now I know what narcissism is. I wish I'd known about it before. I feel so stupid after getting involved with him, but now I realise it has happened to a lot of other women - women who were all intelligent and successful.

Apparently, they prowl around, looking for women like us. Anyway, it has helped me stop blaming myself."

Kate nodded, "I know the counsellor that you went to for help, and I told her what happened. I told her you did not feel you were listened to."

"I am glad you did that," Joanna replied vindicated; "I don't want to see her, or any other counsellor, ever again."

Kate brought out a bottle of red wine, which Joanna recognised from the label. "That was mine!" she said, shaking her head.

"He turned around and gave it to me. Let's have a toast with OUR wine," Kate said, uncorking the bottle.

Laughing, they drank toasts and mocked Silver-tongue.

Returning home, Joanna found that the curtain to the back door window was missing. Frightened, she unlocked the door to find it lying on the floor. The curtain wire had disappeared. Nothing else was missing apart from that. Baffled, she shook her head. What did that mean? Had Silver-tongue been in the house? If it was him, how did he get in, and why would he have taken the curtain wire? The sight of the shepherd crook standing guard by the coal range reassured her.

Joanna talked to Kate often in the weeks that followed. It helped them recover from their involvement with Silver-tongue.

Silver-tongue had over-reached himself with Kate. Gregarious, outgoing and talkative, she had a wide network of informants.

Kate soon found out the truth about Silver-tongue and his wife that Joanna had been unable to uncover, and she told everyone.

Embarrassed she'd not been able to find out the truth like Kate had, Joanna felt like a fool. She'd tried for three years to find out the truth, but didn't have many friends locally, and Silver-tongue was a secretive man who kept to himself. She'd never met any of his friends.

She did not want her involvement with Silver-tongue to be made common knowledge, but Kate spread it far and wide. Joanna felt very uncomfortable, feeling that it came very close to salacious gossip. What price did she have to pay for the truth?

When she spoke to the King about it, he replied; *"Whoever walks in integrity walks securely, but whoever takes crooked paths will be found out." Proverbs 10:9 (NIV)*

"Secrecy was his biggest advantage. I wanted the truth to bring you some closure. I am sorry you have been the subject of gossip, but it will save the next woman he's targeted."

The King continued; "I know what made him choose his ways, whereas you can only guess at the reasons. I have heard it talked over between the two of you. You are straying into judgement. I want you to become a good judge of character and have discernment, but leave the evil people to me."

"Do not be like children in your thinking my friends; be children so far as evil is concerned, but be grown up in your thinking." 1 Corinthians 14:20 (GNT)

"As I live,' says the Lord GOD, 'I have no pleasure in the death of the wicked, but that the wicked turn from his way and live." Ezekiel 33:11 (NKJ)

View from the mountain

"No soap can wash away my sins," (Job 9:30) Joanna said rather despondently as she scrubbed at herself in the shower. A season had passed since Joanna had fought free of Silver-tongue, but she still felt filthy from her involvement with him. She kept these feelings to herself.

The Minstrel, who didn't know she'd spoken these words to the King, brought her a gift for her birthday. It was soap, bearing these words; "*God is Love*" *(1 John 4:8)*

Joanna smiled at the King but read no more from the gift than that. The Minstrel blew hot and cold in friendship. She put it down to his temperament. It did not occur to her until afterwards that they always seemed to get on better together when White Flower was not around.

Was he the one the King had promised? They did not seem to be compatible. She decided to get to a higher place to see the land.

One Sunday morning on the second year of her journey, Joanna stood in the little church on the hill where she lived, worshipping the King with this song;

I see the King standing on the Mountain
I see Him clearer each day
I see the King standing on the Mountain
And He says "Prepare Ye the Way."

The song led her into the Kingdom, where she found herself on a mountain top. Her eyes widened as she glimpsed the King in all his beauty and viewed a land that stretched afar.

The princess within came forth and joined the King, looking back along the path she had struggled up. The Valley of Shadow lay in the distance. Down below the crooked path disappeared into the wilderness like an ugly scar. It joined the wide road leading to the dragon's dark kingdom.

A narrow path skirted the bad-lands, snaking up into impassable looking mountains on a shadowy horizon. She spied a desert in the distance that she hoped she would not have to cross.

Standing by her side, the King said "I have stopped you here before I lead you on to acknowledge and encourage you. When we started out, I had to lift you, and carry you. Now you are walking with me."

"Albeit in a somewhat zig-zag fashion" Joanna joked.

He smiled.

Glowing in the warmth of his smile, she thanked him. "It is only because of you that I have got this far! I can't make the journey without you" she said.

The Lord said, "You are one of mine - called out of the fire and flood; called to be an overcomer. You now have a choice. I will ask you to walk with me on hard yet interesting paths, where everything I give you will be tested, or you can settle down under my protection and still have my blessing. Which path do you choose?"

Joanna regarded the King with a smile, liking the word "choose".

"I'll take the high road, the hard yet interesting path," she replied, choosing the path of wisdom.

"Then who do you choose to walk with, among the men of my people?" the Lord asked.

She smiled, "I thought you had already *chosen* him."

He said "I have. Now you must ask for him. As yet, he is out of sight. Ask and he shall be given to you."

Reflecting on how she had changed, Joanna said "It is good that you promise me this, Lord. I was getting worried about how I have changed. I can't go back to where I used to be. You have taught me to think with your mind, which separates me from men outside of your Kingdom. I know to them I would now appear strange and different - and I feared I would have to remain alone.

While I know I can enjoy the friendship of men who don't know you, I also know I can't marry them, for how can I be yoked together with an unbeliever?

Can two walk together, except they are agreed? Amos 3:3 (KJV)

I know I am no more righteous than an unbeliever, but my right standing before the Father now comes from you. I know I can't get right with you by keeping the law - and good deeds don't outweigh the bad. My own righteousness is as filthy rags. It is your Kingdom I seek; and your righteousness."

She paused. "I ask for one who will be my equal in your Kingdom. One who knows you, bows to you, is taught by you, understands scripture, wears armour, has conquered the dragon in bloody battles - yet laughs easily, is good with my children and can make me laugh."

The King nodded.

She said slowly, "Um, Lord ..."

"Yes?" the King replied, waiting.

"I know I'm not supposed to judge on outward appearances, but can he please by easy on the eye as well?"

"A handsome prince?" the King asked, raising an eyebrow.

Joanna paused, wondering if the King was going to tell her not to judge on outward appearances. "Yes, but that is the least important, and I will trust you in this."

The King smiled. She hadn't mentioned money.

Chapter Four

Groaning inwardly, Joanna stared into her coffee mug as she sat on her veranda listening to the Minstrel moan about life as a single parent. It was discouraging. He wasn't a special case. She was leading a family by herself *and* working. She wished for the man the King had promised her, but there was no sign of him.

The King had said that he was out of sight. He certainly was. Perhaps it was because he did not exist. Perhaps she'd imagined the King's promise. Her thoughts led to discouragement and worry about the future.

She knew that the Minstrel wasn't the one the King had promised, especially after meeting his scary father who believed she was the wife he'd prayed for his son. She had a dream the night after meeting the father, of two bulls butting their heads together. Consulting her dream dictionary, she read "If a woman encounters a bull, she will be likely to receive a proposal of marriage, but she should not accept it." Chuckling, she decided it was a good enough reason to 'steer clear'.

The path led through a place called "the Flatlands" after skirting around the bulls - and their droppings.

The land was bland and featureless, the path flat. She wearily trod through the unendingly monotonous landscape, accompanied by other negative people.

After months of this she cried; "My God, I cannot stand this place anymore! This *must* be the wrong path. Please, help me return to Australia. I know I'll fare better over there!"

Standing by the town's swimming pool the next day, Joanna pondered what to do. She'd asked the King for a prayer partner to replace White Flower, as White Flower's attention was elsewhere.

Lifting her eyes from her daughter happily splashing in the water, she caught the eyes of another watching mother. Her face was becoming familiar as they seemed to take their daughters swimming on the same days. Joanna smiled and moved to sit next to her.

Keeping a watchful eye on their young children, they talked and soon learned they both followed the King.
They smiled at each other in understanding.

"Let's get together for a coffee" Joanna suggested.

Deborah paused as her smile disappeared. Her reply was cautious, "I'd love too, but I cannot invite you to my place. My husband does not like me having friends."

Joanna made a face and said "That sounds familiar. His name's not Hugh, is it?"

"No, who is Hugh?" Deborah asked, smiling at the look on Joanna's face.
"A man who didn't like *me* having friends," Joanna replied; "I called him 'Silver-tongue' after the term 'Silver-tongued devil'. I finally got shot of him last year. You can come back to my place. I promise you it is safe. The house is under the watchful eye of the King."

Knowing they had each other's back they soon became firm friends. Deborah did not gossip, which Joanna needed and was glad of.
She came to trust Deborah when the things they shared stayed between them. Deborah appreciated Joanna's knowledge of the rough terrain of her marriage.
"I will support you whatever you choose to do, whether you stay with your husband, or leave him," Joanna promised.

Both women had their battles. Deborah often found herself abused, belittled and undermined by her second husband.

Joanna knew what that felt like and had a heart for Deborah.

Although she found it hard to trust others, especially men, she did not want her experiences with Silver Tongue to taint or prejudice the way she saw Deborah's husband.

They learned they'd both been given the same word by the King, *"to rebuild the temple."*

The Riddler had given Joanna that word, but he often delivered words that were cryptic and pitched well into the future, in this case a year's advance march. She knew it meant they needed to rebuild their lives according to the King's will and design.

How were they going to do that? It occupied much of their discussion as they walked the road of righteousness together.

The King heard them. Standing in front of a lit candlestick with seven lamps and seven channels, he said;
"You will succeed, not by might, not by power, but by my spirit. Obstacles as great as mountains, will disappear before you."
Zechariah 4:6 (GNT)

The second wish

Inside, the kitchen was cool in the heat of the day. The Minstrel was outside painting Joanna's house. She had contracted him to do the work as he was a painter by trade. He was taking weeks to do the job, bringing his children over to play each day while he worked. The children's laughter filtered into the house as they played outside on the lawn.

White Flower, a regular visitor, arrived with her children. Tired of the Minstrel being at her place every day, Joanna was mulling over a holiday.
"I'm thinking about going away on holiday for a week or two. If I give you the keys, can you keep an eye on the place?" she asked.
"Yes, I can do that," White Flower responded, "When are you going?"

Suddenly they stopped talking as the light in the room changed. The Minstrel had stretched himself out across the kitchen window pane while painting the window surrounds.

Clad only in brief shorts, his nipples were firmly pressed against the glass. White Flower laughed and Joanna grimaced. Didn't he know women were not visual?
"Now you can see why I've had enough of him. I'll leave tomorrow" Joanna replied irritated.

The Minstrel had been goading her with snide little put downs, but always through White Flower, and Joanna was tired of it.

Packing that night, she talked to the King, "I've seen how White Flower flirts with the Minstrel and other men. She enjoys male attention, even though she's married. How is it she can feel confident and attract men - and here I am feeling so bad about myself?"

Looking up from his book, the King answered, "My reply to you and White Flower is that your true beauty should consist of a gentle and quiet spirit."

She sighed, "Yes, Lord ... and I suppose you are going to tell me it is in your word - and for me to look it up."

The King smiled, "Yes, it is in my word;
'Instead, your beauty should consist of your true inner self, the ageless beauty of a gentle and quiet spirit, which is of the greatest value in God's sight.'" 1 Peter 3:4 (GNT)

"Why are you are feeling so jaded?" he asked.

She replied, "The men in my life ... especially the ones in this story, have all been masters at putting me down, or putting me last."

"Forget them for a moment. Stop looking at yourself through their eyes. How do *you* see yourself?" the King asked, holding her eyes.

"I've been told I'm attractive. My face is not too long like my mother said.

Women are equal to men, despite what my father and Silver-tongue have said, but ..." she replied, her words trailing off.

"But?" the King prompted.

" I don't *feel* attractive."

"You are suffering from low self-esteem. From childhood you've had a damaged self-image, which Silver-tongue exploited to his advantage," the King replied.

He wanted Joanna to see herself through his eyes as a princess - a woman of ageless beauty, possessing the genuine charm of a gentle and quiet spirit.

Joanna nodded "Yes – and when the Minstrel puts me down it reminds me of Silver-tongue.

I think he builds himself up by tearing others down. I want to walk away from the friendship. He's not important to me, but the children's friendship is. Please bring me someone who sees me for who I really am and who desires me."

Raising an eyebrow like he did the last time she'd made a wish, the King looked at his scepter as if to ask "Do you think this is a fairy wand?"

Why was she not asking him for the man he'd promised?

"Be careful what you ask for" he remarked, knowing she was reacting instead of thinking ahead.

She didn't hear him.

The circle begins

Opportunity knocked in 1997 as the King opened a new door for Joanna, leading her to the start of the circle he'd spoken of at the levelled hill.

The circle began at a school; working in the four storied tower as a Science Technician - a position her friend Eve recommended her for.

The college did not ask about Joanna's science qualifications at the job interview.

"I see you're a computer programmer" the principal said. His rationale was that if she could write code, she could handle the work in the lab. "The job is yours," he said after reading her resume.

Now Joanna had two part time jobs; one as a Science Technician and the other as a Teller at a Credit Union. Delighted, she thanked her friend Eve and the King for the job.

"It's just as well they didn't ask about my science marks!" she said, laughing about the job interview.

Joanna was taken to meet Bret, the Technician she would be replacing, a man with a young face and greying hair.

He looked vaguely familiar. She'd seen him before, somewhere. Where had their paths crossed?

Bret remembered Joanna. They'd done the same computer course - but she'd been in the first year while he'd been in the second.

He remembered a possessive guy who seemed to dog her every move on campus, except for the day he'd seen her alone in the lab with two little children under her desk.

He was all business, staying silent about where he remembered her. Preoccupied, he had a lot of work to get done. He explained he was under a lot of pressure as the school had been expecting him to look after the Science *and* Computer labs.

He was pleasant enough, polite but aloof. Joanna figured he wasn't big on talk, or charm.

Joanna looked around as they walked across the quadrangle. A large elm grew in front of the tower block, its branches reaching to the fourth floor. Yellow and gold leaves were drifting down around them in the cool autumn air.

The lab technician's room on the fourth floor had a beautiful view, looking out over the town towards the hills. Mount Ruapehu, an active volcano, capped the horizon to the north east.

After showing her the two lab rooms and all the equipment, Bret handed over the purchasing book, technician's manual and lab technician's coat.

"Where are you going?" she asked as he prepared to head out the door.

"I don't have time to train you," he said brusquely.

"But, wait ... "she stammered as he held up his hand and shook his head.

"Read the manual," he said over his shoulder before shutting the door.

"What an unfriendly man," she remarked, unused to a man's disinterest.

Shrugging about the lack of training and making a face at the King, she went to work slowly and methodically familiarising herself in the unfamiliar new field.

Dalliance

"Would you like a beer?" the Minstrel asked Joanna, as she dropped her children off to play. It was a sunny autumn afternoon over Easter break.

"Yes, it's hot enough for one" she replied, sitting down on the back door steps to drink it. He came to sit beside her, putting his arm around her. Joanna turned to look at him with her eyebrows raised.

"Probably a million questions are going through your mind right now," the Minstrel said, testing the waters. She hadn't pulled away.

Nodding, Joanna drank her beer and waited for him to explain himself, knowing he was a double-minded man who blew hot and cold. White Flower was away, and that could be the reason they were getting on better. Perhaps he *hadn't* been saying all the things that she'd been repeating.

The other thing that was going through her mind was a bible verse she'd read;
"A friend means well, even when he hurts you. But when an enemy puts his arm around your shoulder - watch out!" Proverbs 27:6 (GNT)

"Are you a friend or enemy?" she asked herself.

"You've been ignoring me and it's made me interested," he drawled.

"Oh really," Joanna replied, annoyed; "I haven't been ignoring you to make you 'interested'. I'm busy with study and two part time jobs, and I'm playing sport again. Go figure."

"You've come a long way since you got rid of the stalker," he replied, mentioning Silver-tongue.

"Uh huh" she replied, wondering where this was going.

Turning his wit and charm on full force, the Minstrel attempted to win Joanna over. She was trying to discern whether this was flattery or this was sincere. Her hungry soul craved for words of affirmation. She found herself interested in spite of her better judgement. Was he finally seeing her for who she really was? Or was there an ulterior motive?

Joanna didn't trust him, but after they put the children to bed, she stayed enjoying the attention, although she kept in mind what the King said about self-control;
"As for you, my brothers, you were called to be free. But do not let this freedom become an excuse for letting your physical desires control you." Galatians 5:13 (GNT)

Keeping him in the friend zone, she walked home leaving her children sleeping at his place. It was his turn to babysit.

"I know it seems far more interesting than the Flat lands, but don't go down that road," the King warned her the next morning.

"I didn't intend any of that. I hadn't even planned to visit him" she answered, yawning and making coffee.

"Why did he act like that? I don't understand the change of heart, and I don't trust him," she remarked.

"You shouldn't" the King replied; "He acts out of his feelings. His moods change as quickly as the Tasman Sea, that ocean out there beyond the river. Do not believe his words."

"You need to stop seeking your worth in the eyes of a man," the King added, knowing her earthly father hadn't carried out his will and given his daughter the love she'd needed.

"Forgive me. I was lonely, I like male company, and I was tempted ..." she answered.

"Watch out," he warned, forgiving her; "*Each person is tempted when they are dragged away by their own evil desire and enticed. Then, after desire has conceived, it gives birth to sin; and sin, when it is full-grown, gives birth to death." James 1:14-15.*

The Crossroads

Staring moodily out the window of her tower, Joanna finished her work. The sky was as dark as the expression on her face. She would have to pick her children up from school soon.

Normally she enjoyed the three o'clock school pickup. It was the time of the day when she could meet up with her friends - but lately it had become oppressive. Gossip hung in the air like a toxic vapour. It was coming from the house directly over the road from the school - the house Cherry had recently moved into.

Joanna had been friends with Cherry in her early teens ... until the weekend she'd found her in bed with her thirteen-year-old brother. Even though it had happened more than twenty years ago, she had not forgotten. She didn't trust her and feared there'd be trouble.

Her fears were realised. Although Cherry had a boyfriend, she was also seeing the Minstrel. She lapped his attention up and through White Flower accused Joanna of being jealous. It was a slap in the face for Joanna, who had no time for Cherry.

Joanna didn't want to marry the Minstrel; they were too different. But she liked his companionship and wanted to keep the friendship. He was the only male companion she had. Her father and brother were dead and all her other male friends were in

Sydney.

The Minstrel and White Flower were now spending most of their time at Cherry's place. Isolated, Joanna felt as if her friends were being stolen from her.

It seemed the Lord was using Cherry as a human wrecking ball. Joanna faced the facts; if Cherry could wreck things that easily they weren't good relationships in the first place.

"It's time to let go. Walk away. Draw near to me and I will draw near to you," the King said compassionately, turning his face toward her and reaching for the hurt child within.
"Soon you will be coming up to a crossroads. Ask for the ancient path," he advised.

'Stand at the crossroads and look. Ask for the ancient paths and where the best road is. Walk in it, and you will live in peace.'
Jeremiah 6:16 (GNT)

Joanna had not yet arrived at the crossroads. Not knowing what the Lord meant, she focused on the immediate problem - what to do about the deep ties between her children and the Minstrel's children, when it was becoming intolerable for her to remain in a friendship with their father.

Tired of the mind games, she went to see the Minstrel. Going into the lion's den, she faced him down and told him what she expected from a friendship.

"I'm at a crossroads," he said, surprising Joanna.

"So am I, it seems" she replied tersely.

Although Joanna had written the Minstrel out of the Kingdom story, she foolishly thought he should have the part of the story where he had appeared in it, before she walked away. It would explain things for his father.

"The Kingdom is real," she told him "The King is real. You can follow him and have a fairy tale, or you can go your way and have a soap opera."

The Minstrel did not understand. In his ego and pride, he did not realize they'd be parting company at the crossroads.

It was then that he dropped a bombshell, casually informing her he'd merely amused himself with her while waiting for another woman to turn up after Easter. She froze. An enemy had put his arm around her shoulder!

Joanna recoiled. "I don't like being used" she said flatly, looking at him with hatred. Putting him in the same mental rubbish bin as Silver-tongue, she placed the lid down hard.

He shrugged the words off as if they didn't matter.

"How about we do something over the school holidays?" he asked, as she walked out the door.

Joanna was shocked at his callous attitude and deeply offended. Couldn't he see how angry she was?

"I'm busy" she replied dismissively, as she pulled on her boots and walked out of his life.

The children could play together, but Mum and Dad wouldn't be. The princess within closed the gate and raised the drawbridge.

Watching them, the King said; *"A brother offended is harder to win than a strong city, and contentions are like the barred gates of a citadel."* (Proverbs 18:19)

Pearls to pigs

The hill Joanna lived on used to be called Mars Hill, and Mars was an old Roman god of war. It was a name for conflict if there ever was one. Mount Ruapehu seemed to agree as it belched out ash and smoke. A fight loomed large on the horizon.

After the school holidays, Joanna crossed paths with the Minstrel. She had seen him come out the gate from Cherry's house while picking the children up after school. She knew from White Flower they'd been gossiping about her again and she grew even angrier. White Flower had gleefully lapped up the gossip at Cherry's place, making sure Joanna heard *all* the things he had to say about her.

Seeing the look on Joanna's face, the King said *"Gossip brings anger just as surely as the north wind brings rain."*
Proverbs 25:23 GNT

The gossip burned in her ears as she walked past the Minstrel, who looked smug. He was the king of the hill, and believed all the women wanted him – especially Joanna.

Feeling sure of himself, he spoke to Joanna in a patronizing manner. If he'd kept silent, Joanna would have ignored him, but now he'd gotten her attention.

Seething, she stopped to glare at him, her eyes shooting sparks and boulders. "Listen. I don't respect you. Leave me alone. Stay away from me!" she snapped, walking off.
Unprepared for her anger, the Minstrel staggered back with a look of shock and dismay. She'd stung him hard.

Joanna knew the King would not approve of her retaliating this way, but it had come unbidden. It was in her nature to sting if trodden upon. Pleased at the hurt she'd inflicted, she was sure it would only be a hurt to his ego, which needed readjusting anyway.

The Minstrel thought Joanna was a forgiving person. And she'd given him what he'd interpreted as a love story.

Believing everything White Flower had gossiped about, he never stopped to think about how Joanna might be feeling or how low her opinion of him might have gotten. Joanna had trusted White Flower to set him straight, only realising much later that White Flower had her own agenda - and would have played them all off against each other.
There is a proverb that says *"A perverse man stirs up dissension, and a gossip separates close friends." (Proverbs 16:28).*

How true it was. It seemed the Minstrel had stirred it up and White Flower had dished it out.

Joanna approached the King;
"You know that I've been writing this story as it happens,"
The King nodded; "Uh-huh ..."

"Before the Minstrel told me what he'd done at Easter, I gave him a copy of the chapters where he appeared. When I gave the Minstrel his part in the Kingdom story, I gave him the good parts and the bad parts. I wanted him to respect my journey.

It was in answer to his father's designs for me, thinking I was the answer to his prayers.
I thought I made it clear that we would be parting company if he could not treat me with respect.

I said I wanted to be left in peace - and not be bothered by deceitful men. It was my line in the sand."

The King nodded again as she ploughed on; "Well, it was a mistake. His ego is wounded. Now he has gone and shown his mother, Cherry and only you know who else the story. Without context, it will be interpreted any old way he wants it to be, no doubt to bolster his own self-image. I'll bet he didn't show them the part where I called him a toad!"

She waited. It was hard to gauge the Lord's expression.

He replied, "*Your people are talking about you when they meet by the city walls or in the doorways of their houses. They say to one another, 'Let's go and hear what word has come from the Lord now.' To them you are nothing more than an entertainer singing love songs or playing a harp.*" Ezekiel 33:30-32 (GNT)

"I did not write the story to entertain the small-town gossips!" Joanna replied in exasperation and disgust; "Why did they even read it or talk about it? How is this any of their business?

It was between me and him - and you know I didn't intend it as a love story!"

"Nor did Ezekiel, the prophet this word was about," the King replied. "Do not be discouraged. I want you to treat this as a learning experience. What would have happened if my prophets had given up delivering the word that I gave? I want you to carry on writing about the Kingdom."

"I am a seeker, not a prophet," she replied shaking her head.

"Why, oh why did I think *you* wanted me to give him the story of the Kingdom where he appeared in it?

Where was my head at? What was I thinking? It has only led to trouble!" she exclaimed.

"How do you know this wasn't my will?" the King asked. "You were both at the crossroads," he reminded her, adding "This is not just about you. The temptations in life are no different from what others experience. And I am faithful.

Your story about the Kingdom is my story. It is about me, belongs to me, and to those who seek me. It needs to be shared, for I will use it to speak to others."

"Remember this though, *'Do not give dogs what is sacred; do not throw your pearls to pigs. If you do, they may trample them under their feet, and then turn and tear you to pieces'"*
Matthew 7:6 (NIV)

The King had never said a truer word.

Agreeing, Joanna had a little dig at him; "Okay, I was dumb. But I have a question for you. How is it that *you* can call him a pig, but *I* can't call him a toad?"

"Well, if we *are* talking about fairy tales, now you see what happens to a pig when the princess kisses him," the King replied, amused at the question.
"What happens?" Joanna asked.

The King showed her a pig grunting in the mud and she got it.
"He's still a pig!" she exclaimed, laughing at the King's wisecrack and feeling a lot better.
"Yes, he's still a pig" the King replied, "but look closer."

The pig had a gold ring in its nose.
"*Like a gold ring in a pig's snout is a beautiful woman who shows no discretion*" he advised, quoting a proverb from Proverbs 11:22.
"Ouch" she said.
"No experience is wasted," he reassured her, "In future you will learn to judge wisely and objectively so you can avoid embarrassment or distress," he promised.

In the days that followed Joanna had to endure slander attacks from the Minstrel, the one who she had counted as a friend. Yet she had not done him any wrong. His mother and a friend joined in the fray, even though it did not concern them. Joanna was astonished to see he'd gone crying to his mother. It was like a divorce!

The King sent his trusted servant Livia to her. Livia knew how to fight dragons. Coming and going from up north, Livia had kept a watchful eye on Joanna and the children ever since the days of the Pits. Now Livia had recently made her home in the same town as Joanna. Joanna needed a healthy friend and Livia had become her mentor.

"Help, I am getting attacked by all these dragons!" Joanna told Livia.

"You are better off without him for a friend," Livia said, not surprised. "He was not a safe person.
Do you not know that the King promises a blessing for the times when you are attacked like this? Listen to these words from the King;

'Blessed are you when people insult you, persecute you and falsely say all kinds of evil against you because of me. Rejoice and be glad, because great is your reward in heaven,
For in the same way they persecuted the prophets who were before you.'" Matthew 5:11 (NIV)

"Thanks, but I do not see this as a blessing ..." Joanna muttered.

"It will be okay," Livia reassured her, "You'll get through this and he'll be replaced by healthy friends."
Joanna frowned. "I can't wait. What about the children?" she asked anxiously, adding, "I doubt they're going to play together anymore!"

"You've got to be safe," Livia replied, shaking her head; "It was too much of a price to pay for them to play together. They'll find other friends."

The House of the Fathers

From the crossroads, the road in the Kingdom was shrouded in mist. Joanna couldn't discern any signposts.

Feeling weary and fed up with people, Joanna asked, "What do I do now Lord?"

The Lord replied;
"Let your eyes look straight ahead, Fix your gaze directly before you. Make level paths for your feet, and take only ways that are firm. Do not swerve to the right or the left; Keep your foot from evil." Proverbs 4:25-27 (NIV)

Remembering that she had to find the ancient paths, she asked;
"Please show me the ancient paths and where the best road is, so that I may walk in it, and live in peace." (Jeremiah 6:16)

Extending his hand to her, the King led Joanna to an avenue of oaks. The road was beautiful at this part, where the trees formed an arch overhead. The sign said 'Oak Road'.
Coincidentally it was the name of the road that led to her childhood farm near Napier, but there had been no oaks in the time she lived there.

They walked through the avenue to a place the King called 'the house of the Fathers'. Entering the house, they walked into a study lined with books, where she saw herself receiving the family Bible from her father before he died.

It had been handed down for generations, ever since Anna, the family matriarch had given it to Walter, her son. Joanna's eyes met the eyes of her earthly father as they spoke without words. Joanna knew her father was dying.

"I will take care of it," she promised. Her brother should have been carrying this. It felt so heavy.

Knowing how wounded she'd been in her father's house, the Lord said;

"Listen, daughter, and pay careful attention, forget your people and your father's house. Let the king be enthralled by your beauty; honour him, for he is your lord." (Psalm 45:10-11)

Joanna saw a fireplace in the study of her father's house. The fire had gone out long ago.

Her heart felt as dry as the ashes.

"I will give beauty for ashes," the King promised;

*"I will comfort all who mourn, and provide for those who grieve in Zion, to bestow on them a crown of beauty instead of ashes, the oil of joy instead of mourning, and a garment of praise instead of a spirit of despair. You will be called oaks of righteousness, a planting of the LORD for the display of my splendor.
You will renew that which has been devastated for generations - building the old wastes and raising up the former desolations, the desolations of many generations." (Isaiah 61:3-4)*

Rebuilding the wall

Leaning back in her chair, Joanna looked at her friend Deborah. They were reading the book of Nehemiah; the man instrumental in the rebuilding of Jerusalem following the Babylonian exile.

"So, we've both been given the word to 'rebuild the temple'. How do we do what Nehemiah did in real life?" she asked.

"You can start with the wall, like Nehemiah did," the King replied, "I will provide guidance on how to rebuild your lives.

We'll start with boundaries. I want you to visualise your boundaries as being a fence, a stone wall around you."

Before the week was out, he brought books and audio on building boundaries. He came to join Joanna, who was sprawled out amongst the building material, listening to the tapes and taking notes from a book on Boundaries by Dr. Henry Cloud and Dr. John Townsend.

He explained the wrong done; "*As a child you were taught that setting boundaries or saying no was wrong; and as a consequence you believed that others could do with you as they wished.*
You were sent defenseless into a world of controlling, manipulative, and exploitative people. Your ability to say no was blocked, and it had handicapped you for life.

You said yes to bad things, through fear of disobeying a harsh conscience. It made you unable to confront others, because it caused guilt.

Not only did it keep you from refusing evil in your life, it often kept you from recognising evil. Your spiritual and emotional radar was broken; you had no ability to guard her heart."

"No wonder I've had so much trouble with bad people," Joanna replied; "I wish I'd known this years ago.

Hey, look what it says here; *"Boundaries are for keeping the temple secure. Boundaries are freedom, and freedom is love. Boundaries are not for giving justice to someone who is a jerk."*

She laughed about the word 'jerk.'

"I will tear down the house of the proud, but establish the boundary of the widow" the King promised, using a proverb from Proverbs 15:25.

"The books and audio are confirming everything you're telling us," Joanna said, thrilled at his guidance.

Smiling, the King said "I have watched you through all the long hours of study you did to earn your bread in the world. Now you are finally learning what I've been longing to teach you! I am delighted when people desire to learn from me. I will honour that and teach them."

The King helped them rebuild their lives. They learned about damaged boundaries in families. He outlined his will; *"You are going to be part of a transitional generation that will change direction towards integrity and truthfulness - a generation who will stand firm and not yield to pressure, that will reverse what has been up to ten generations of movement the other way.*

A generation that will say; 'I am going to value the integrity of my spirit, and go the other way.'"

One afternoon Joanna decided to take time out and visit Deborah. Wanting a change from working on boundaries, she wondered what other things they could do in the Kingdom.

The King knew her mind and thought otherwise. The first thing that greeted her as she pulled up at Deborah's was a big pile of rocks. One rock had rolled directly onto the path, while the rest were piled on the grass, waiting. Joanna returned the King's smile as she skirted a boulder.

"Really?" she asked as she walked through the door.

Deborah laughed as she poured a glass of wine for her, explaining that her husband had brought the rocks down from Taupo for landscaping.

Laughing at the big sign they'd been given they made a toast to the King.

Liang

The path of righteousness skirted a field of wildflowers. Joanna parted the long grass, peering into the field. A man with white hair wearing blue jeans and a white shirt was standing there, waiting.

She gazed at him until he was obscured by a branch that gently waved in the air.

Who was he? Was it just her imagination?

A year had passed since Joanna had found herself alone, and she wanted some male companionship.

She wondered whether the King really was going to choose her future husband. What if she'd just imagined him saying it?

It was at this time a bright and confident man she named Liang came into her life. His parents came from China, so he was of a different race even though he was born in the same country.

She liked his pleasant manner and the intelligence that shone from his dark eyes. Joanna did not care about his skin colour, what mattered most was his faith.

Although she did not always keep faith with the King, she respected the King's command not to be yoked with an unbeliever.

"The man I choose must be a follower of the King" she told Liang. "Do you know the Lord?" she asked.
"I know about Him. I am open to Him," he replied.
Joanna thought it sounded positive, and liking him, decided to give him a chance.

Chapter Five

Like Joanna, Liang was learning how to rebuild his life, meeting and studying with people in the world outside the Kingdom. Kate, the woman she helped get away from Silver-tongue, was part of this group. The King was not part of it, although the group had material that tied in with the books and tapes the King had given Joanna.

One night she went with Liang to meet his friends and see what they were learning while rebuilding their lives. She liked what they were doing. They dealt that night with the subject of transitional relationships. A paragraph they read from their book struck her so much she wrote it down;

"Other relationships can help to rebuild, but a pitfall is investing too much emotional time and energy into the new relationship. Learn all you can, heal all you can, and stop holding the precious butterfly in your hands so tightly that it can't fly and be free. The energy you spend holding on tightly to the other person and relationship keeps you from climbing your own mountain and completing your own healing."

As there'd been no scripture for the King to use at Liang's group, he fashioned for Joanna the sign of a butterfly. She did not see the butterfly; instead, she focused her attention on the title of the chapter from the book they'd read.

"That was a useful book they were reading, especially tonight's chapter '*Growing Relationships help me rebuild,*'" she remarked the King, making an assumption; "You brought Liang in to help me rebuild."

The King was patient.
Exercising grace, he ignored the sin of her presumption.
"That was your choice," he merely replied; "Remember that butterflies need to fly."

"Come with me," he said taking her hand; "I want to show you something ..."

Leading her to the field of wildflowers, he showed her a Monarch butterfly that had just emerged from its cocoon.

It alighted on his finger.
"This little butterfly is going to fly for thousands of kilometres, to return to the tree of its great-great grandparents," he said.

"How is that possible?" she wondered, marvelling at his creation.

"They do it in generations - like a relay," he explained; "The first three generations make it in stages, doing their part. The butterfly of the fourth generation looks exactly like all other Monarchs, but they are different. They have to complete the journey."

"How does the butterfly know it is the fourth generation?" she asked, watching the butterfly as it fluttered around them.

"The migrating butterfly knows the time and season it is living in and is given signs, like shorter days and changes in temperature," the King replied.

She was amazed. It seemed an impossible journey for such a fragile creature.

"How can it fly that far?" she asked.

"Don't underestimate it," the King replied; "It will put all of its energy into migrating, and it will find the wind. It will drink nectar and catch warm air currents that will allow it to soar as it goes, instead of having to use its wings."

"How does the butterfly know the tree to return to, when it has never been there?" she asked.

The King smiled, "I created it to *know*."

One night as she talked with Liang, he told her how he centred much of his time around her, so that other things had ceased to be as important to him.

Joanna didn't like it. Silver-tongue used to talk that way, before he turned nasty. Her memory flashed back to the beginning of her 'relationship' with Silver-tongue. Tenderly cupping her face in his hands, Silver-tongue had looked at her with his heart in his eyes.

"You are like a butterfly in a jar" he gently remarked, and she thought he wanted her to be free.

If only she'd known he was a butterfly collector.

Silver-tongue only revealed what he was really thinking to her when they parted.
"I wanted to keep you in *my* jar!" he'd ranted.

To banish the stench of his memory, she sang the snatch of a popular song; "Someone Saved My Life Tonight" by Elton John. "I'm a butterfly, and butterflies are free to fly," she sang, thinking of the Monarch butterfly the King had shown her.

Joanna went back to the decision she made at the start of the relationship with Liang. He was aware she needed a man who followed the King. She made no bones about that, it was non-negotiable.

Liang said he had opened the door to the King, but Joanna did not see a change of heart, or observe very much interest in the King.

"Where are you headed?" she asked Liang.

"I don't know," he replied.

"Well, who leads you then?" she asked, frowning.

"No-one. I make the decisions for myself," he replied.

"So, how do you now regard the Lord?" Joanna asked.

"I am being polite to him, while I try to make my mind up" he replied, still in the place where they had first met, sitting on the fence.

It wasn't what Joanna wanted to hear.
Lifting her eyes from her work, she looked out of the lab window at the mountain which crowned the horizon.
Joanna realised her own mountain awaited her in the journey toward healing. Although Liang had helped, he could not heal her heart. She would have to leave him sitting on the fence and keep climbing.

Would the path be higher and more rugged than the paths she'd tramped on the mountain framed in her window? She suspected it would be.

A mountain waited to be climbed and a butterfly waited to be free.

The winds of change

It was a time of change. Joanna was about to embark on a full-time job in her chosen career. It was a good job, and no one would ever know the massive hurdles she'd overcome to win it. After the first interview, she had to sit an IQ test.

"You can do it" Liang encouraged her.

"I can't" she said miserably; "I tried to get that job years ago, and failed the math part of the test."

The King wanted her to try again. He reminded her of a passage from 'The Power of Positive Thinking' by Norman Vincent Peale, a book he had given her at the start of her journey;

"Whatever you're doing, give it all you've got. Give every bit of yourself. Hold nothing back. Life cannot deny itself to the person who gives life his all. Throw your heart over your difficulty, throw your affirmation over every barrier, and throw your visualization over your obstacles. Throw your heart over the bar and your body will follow."

Would the King bring her back to this place if she could not overcome it?

The day of the IQ test came. The room was full of people, as it had been years ago. As she nervously took her place, she affirmed to herself *"I can do all things through the power of Christ who strengthens me."* Philippians 4:13 (NKJ)

Throwing her heart over the bar, she rose to the challenge, passing the test and winning the job ahead of all the other applicants. The King had taken her from failure to victory.

Joanna was elated.

With the approach of the year 2000, she was about to join a worldwide army of computer programmers who were needed to change the two-bit date fields in computer programs to four bits. Otherwise, computer programs would crash when the year 2000 was subtracted from the year 1999.

She wanted to tell her family, but came back down to earth with a thud. There was no-one to call. She rang her mentor with the good news, but Livia wasn't happy.

"But this is what I've spent the last three years studying for! Why are you so disapproving?" Joanna asked, robbed of her joy.

"It's too early to go back to full-time work. Your children need you." Livia replied.

Doubt set in. It meant giving up her room at the tower, and her other part time job. It meant not having as much time with her children.

Standing at the threshold anxious and afraid, she asked herself "What if Livia is right? What if this is *not* what the King wants for me? What if I find I cannot do the job, after I have committed myself to it?"

She reminded herself how she'd sought the King's will before winning the job. Would the door have opened if it was against his will?

Before they parted, Liang took her to a meeting of the King in the town where he lived. In the meeting, a man spoke out the King's word, saying; "Never think that you cannot do it. You CAN do it, for I the Lord AM with you. When you commit your way to me, it WILL succeed."

Afterwards, Liang said "I think that message was for you."

She knew in her heart he was right.

The rock face

The Lord pondered the path Joanna had taken.

Lightly tapping her with His shepherd's staff, he led her back to the road. Warning her to be careful to follow it, he said *"Give careful thought to the paths for your feet and be steadfast in all your ways." (Proverbs 4:26)*

Joanna heard what the King was saying. Knowing she'd taken a bit of a detour with Liang, it was time to make a decision. Liang knew what she wanted - she'd been clear about that from the start. Theirs was a transitional relationship; and she'd gone as far with him as she could.

She stopped seeing Liang when her new career began in January 1998. Their parting was easy and amicable.

Following the King back to road, she skirted the field of wildflowers. The butterfly fluttered above, flying free.

Joanna looked forward to where the road would take her now.

The new job did not start off well. Having looked forward to this stage of the journey with so much excitement, fear, trepidation and hope, Joanna regretted it instantly.

She found herself in a hostile place where there was no time for newcomers. The work was challenging. It was like climbing a vertical rock face, with nothing to grab onto.

She'd been given the workplace bully for a mentor, and the sabotage began immediately.

Treated with contempt and disrespect, bewildered, humiliated, and intimidated, Joanna hung on to the job for grim death.

"How am I ever going to learn?" she asked herself in distress.

Joanna did not know how to confront the bully, and there was no support around her. Her unhelpful colleagues, who'd been there for twenty years, did not want to share their knowledge.

It was a familiar and lonely place. It had been like this at home, at school, in the workplaces outside Australia, and with Silver-Tongue. Would the abuse never end?

"The fault must be with *me*. I must deserve this," she thought with a feeling of despair.

Digging deep, she reminded herself of the hard places she'd been before. It would get better once she gained the knowledge and could prove herself. She would not be defeated. Her will was to succeed and come out stronger.

What was the King's will? Where was his favour? He was silent in the face of the abuse. Had she chosen the wrong job?

"Relent Lord; teach me and establish the work of my hands for me"; she pleaded her cause with the King, as she set her face like flint.

"For the Lord GOD will help me; therefore shall I not be confounded: therefore have I set my face like a flint, and I know that I shall not be ashamed.
Isaiah 50:7 (KJV)

My days may come to seventy years, or eighty, if my strength endures; yet the best of them are but trouble and sorrow, for they quickly pass, and I will fly away.
If only I knew the power of your anger! Your wrath is as great as the fear that is your due.
Teach me to number my days; that I may gain a heart of wisdom.
Relent, LORD! How long will it be? Have compassion on me your servant.

Satisfy me in the morning with your unfailing love; that I may sing for joy and be glad all my days.
Make me glad for as many days as you have afflicted me, for as many years as I have seen trouble.
May your deeds be shown to your servant, your splendor to my children.
May your favour oh Lord my God rest on me; establish the work of my hands for me—
yes, establish the work of my hands." Psalm 90:10-17 (NIV)

Doubt, and the King's answer

The bullying environment led to the desert. Resigning herself to that arid place, Joanna went back to survival mode where dreams were forbidden. She'd endured too much abuse to trust the King's promise.

Whoever and wherever the promised man was, he was not at the company she'd joined.

Perhaps he did not exist. Joanna knew one of the men at her company was cheating on his wife, and she did not trust many of the others either.
*"Help, Lord, for the godly are now more; the faithful have vanished from among men.
Everyone lies to his neighbour; their flattering lips speak with deception." (Psalm 12:1-2)*

One day she met her friend Eve at a café in an old Victorian building. Eve knew the King, but did not trust him when it came to matters of the heart. Their lunchtime discussion had veered into men, love, and relationships.

"I no longer believe in love. Even if I did, what good would it do?" Joanna told Eve.
"I believed; therefore I spoke, I am greatly afflicted, I said in my haste, all men are liars. Psalm 116:10-11 (NKJ)

"What about Liang?" Eve asked.

"He was a good man;" Joanna acknowledged, "But not a follower of the King. While he treated me well, I discovered that transitional relationships do not lead to healing. The scars remain."

"Yes, that is a shame. I know you have grown very cynical." Eve remarked.

"Better a dry crust in a house full of peace than a banquet in a house full of trouble," Joanna replied, quoting from Proverbs 17:1.

Unseen by them, the King heard every word. He gave her a message that night, one she would never forget.

That evening Joanna and her children had gone across the road to their neighbor's place, to meet with the circle of friends she'd surrounded herself with after leaving the crossroads.

Most of them lived on the hill near her, and they met once a week for a shared meal. The fellowship was born from the faith they all shared in the King. Joanna realised they were all survivors of abuse – but that was not what it was about.

They were people from different backgrounds who drew strength from each other and their relationship with the King.

Eve was not part of this group, so no-one knew what had been discussed at lunch. After dinner they sat in the lounge, passing a paper around the circle called 'Discerning genuine love.'

Everyone got a different paragraph to read out, about genuine love. White Flower's message was *"It does not seek its own"* which Joanna thought very appropriate.

White Flower had to read out; *"It does not pursue selfish advantage. It does not have primary concern for sexual appetites or social status but concern for the needs of the one (being dated) and the families involved."*

When it came to her, Joanna was startled to find hers was *"It hopes all things."*
She read out; *"It knows no fading of its hope. It is not fickle. It has perfect peace and confidence that God is primarily responsible for introducing the right partner at the right time."*

The King met her eyes. He didn't have to say anything. She knew.

He said; "It will be to you according to your belief. Do not doubt my promise."

'Hope deferred makes the heart grow sick, but a longing fulfilled is a tree of life.' Proverbs 13:12 (NIV)

Joanna took the hope the King extended to her that night as a precious gift.

Hope was released. Hope as strong and as frail as the butterfly she'd seen fluttering through the Kingdom on its way to the tree of life.

Carefully folding the paper, she kept it against the times when she would be assailed by doubt. Feeling bad about her lack of faith, Joanna repented and apologised, "Lord, I am sorry. I was wrong. In my mind I felt beaten, but pessimistically I will cling to hope!"

'I believe. Help thou my unbelief,' Mark 9:24 (NKJ)

The Father

Joanna settled into a routine, seeing her friend Deborah every other day, and joining the circle of friends every week for fellowship and a shared meal.

She told herself it was better to *be* alone, rather than be with someone who made her *feel* alone.

Rob was one of the Circle of Friends; a tall man of mixed Maori and European ancestry. He earned a living as an entertainer with his rich singing voice. A natural leader, he had *mana* - the Maori word for authority, but at times he could be stubborn and inflexible. His wife Nina was graceful and friendly and a good mother to their little girl.

"Do you think this is all there is; and all that the Father has for you?" Rob challenged her; "Daughter of the King, he is your father! When the little princess gives you a hug, you always reciprocate. The Father wants you to receive, *without* having to reciprocate."

She shrugged. What was he on about? Her heart said; "I don't know how."

About to dismiss what Rob was saying, she was stopped by the memory of the day she'd first heard God speak; when he'd showed himself to her as a father with a baby, and he'd tenderly spoken to her from the book of Hosea.

Was God the Father only like that with babies? What about older children, she wondered?

The tenderness she'd seen brought her back to the whole Father thing. Sometimes in her story the King was 'Father', in a rather formal way. Mostly he was the Lord, the King – the one who had to be loved, followed, obeyed, and even feared. But how could God be like a real father? What did that look like?

Brought back to her childhood, she remembered the pessimistic father who had such a negative view of women. When she left his house and made a life for herself, she felt the need to prove herself; over and over. "Look at this!" her sisters said, cleaning out his desk the week after he'd died and finding an old business card of hers from Australia. "He *was* proud of you."

Although he'd softened before his death, it was too late. She'd been either beaten or ignored by her parents while growing up, especially when left by her ill mother to fend for herself.

Even in the midst of a family of eight, she felt alone. Her parents had made her and her brother discipline the younger children, discipline meaning 'thrash.'

In bringing up her own children, she had to reject everything and find her own way, a better way. As a mother she'd been different in every way that counted; loving them with fairness, firmness and applying loving discipline when necessary.

Joanna went to the Father feeling angry and cheated; "I do not know your love, only the back of your hand."

The Father tried reaching out again, but she retreated from him.

"I will call you Lord" she offered instead.

He waited.

Joanna could see the Father wasn't going away.

"This Father-Daughter thing ... I don't know how to relate to you that way! Can't we just keep it as ..." she trailed off.

"As what?" he asked compassionately.

"I'm happy to be a Servant" she offered.

"The foundation has to be built on the father-daughter relationship," he insisted, gently but firmly.

The dragon appeared, clothed in invisibility and disguised as 'thought.'

He was very rational as he brought up the issue of her brother's death; "How can you rely on him as a father, when he let your only brother die?"

She didn't want to listen to the dragon, but it was true. The King had been deaf to their pleas for help. Sobbing, she buried her head in her arms and put her hands over her ears, crying "Stop! Just stop it."

He did not let up, so she got up and faced him down.

"You did that, Satan. That was your work. My Mother was right when she felt my brother had been murdered. You persecuted him. I saw the confusion, the attack on his soul. You hounded him to death," she said, crying bitterly.

"Yes, and only three weeks after his baptism" he smirked. "You know I can only do what the King permits me to do." Laughing and mocking, he carried on the attack.

Unable to face him any longer, she held her shield over her head and body, reaching for her sword.

Rob was near where she was fighting this dragon.

"Help, I am wrestling with this *thing*," she called out.

Rob did not help her with it.

"You are angry with the King!" he stated.

"What? You started it!" Joanna the warrior princess replied, before withdrawing to fight on her own. "You told me the Father wanted me to receive, without me having to give! Help me, don't judge me!"

The fight with the dragon, the lack of compassion and the weight of being judged wore her out. Clang! Her shield rattled from another attempted blow by the dragon, but the one that felled her came from the club wielded by Rob.

Afterward she went to the King, throwing down her badly dented shield and smoking armour.

"Please, I can't deal with being your daughter! Isn't it enough that I'll believe in you and follow you? Forgive me, but if I take up my place in your Kingdom as your daughter, the dragon will come back. He'll fight me with logic and I don't have an answer. There's no remedy for my pain, except to choose not to go there."

The Father's eyes mirrored her hurt. "I'm not asking you to give what you do not have," he appealed. "It is not about what *I* need, it is about what *you* need. I want you to receive a gift. It will be freely given, but a gift serves no purpose if a person will not receive it!"

Joanna replied "I already have salvation."

The Father could see he wasn't getting through to her. "The dragon wants to cheat you out of your inheritance," he said.

"My inheritance?" she blurted out confused. No-one had taught her about this.

"Lord, I believe you want me to see something I'm blind to," Joanna said, moved and mystified; "I thought salvation was enough. Now I see there is more."
How great is the love the Father has lavished on us, that we should be called children of God! (1 John 3:1)

The Father's Response

The Father spoke; *"I am giving you the spirit of adoption so you can call me Father." (Romans 8:15)*

"For those who are led by the Spirit of God are the children of God. The Spirit you received does not make you slaves, so that you live in fear again; rather, the Spirit you received brought about your adoption to son-ship.

And by him we cry, 'Abba, Father.'" Romans 8:14 (NIV)

"Remember who you are," the Father urged, handing her some letters that her great-great grandmother had written, where the King was called 'Abba.'

She found the letters, and through them a way home to the Father.

Anna wrote; *Ich bete zu den lieben Vater und rufe Abba wie ein kind.*

Reading the translation, Joanna spoke the words; *"I pray to the dear Father and call Abba like a child ..."*

Stumbling over the German, Joanna followed Anna's words in English, words that had been too hard to say on her own;

"Mein Vater ist auch euer Vater."

    "My Father is also your Father."

"sein Vater Herz ist treu gesinnt,"

    "His Fatherly heart is loyal,"

"darum halt Euch,"

    (heart minded faithful)

"getrost an Ihm,"

    "therefore keep your trust in Him,"

"und ruft nur Vater,"

    "and say Father,"

"erhöre doch."

"hear us."

Tears fell as the forgotten German words came to life in English.

Experiencing a moment of deep peace, Joanna spoke to the Father "I pray to you dear Father, and I call you 'Abba' like a child. You are also my father. Your fatherly heart is loyal; heart minded faithful. Therefore, I will keep my trust in you, and I say Father, please hear us."

Unknown to Joanna, a promise that had lain dormant awakened.

"Arise," the Father said; "You did not choose me, I chose you, from eternity. Child of mine, heir to my salvation, you are now a chosen, ransomed, adopted daughter."

Rising to her feet, she played him a song from Fleetwood Mac called 'Oh Daddy.' It was a song she'd always skipped in the past.

Later that week princess Joanna walked into the Kingdom and seated herself before the Father, holding her sword in her lap. The word *"Father"* had a lot more trust in it than *"Lord."*

Troubled, she said "Father, hear me. Forgive me for my lack of faith. It seems so arrogant; you're a King, you're letting me know that I am your daughter, you invite me into a relationship as your daughter, *and I have to decide whether to trust that*?

Here's the thing; I'm accustomed to relating to you as Lord. I thought that's where it begins and ends. It's a relationship where I have an idea of what to expect, and what's expected of me. But this, it's all uncharted territory.

Your Father's love hurts me, pushes me, reaches for me, frightens me, compels me, and I don't know what to expect. I want to be able to *trust you* as my father."

Sighing, she decided on trust "And you don't have to answer to me about my brother's death."

Her eyes got drawn to a booklet that lay next to her sword, with a father holding his baby daughter on the cover. It made her think about the King as a father. She met his gaze.

"I have left a message for you in that booklet," he said.
The message was titled 'When God waits";

When God waits

"My child, I waited for I know more than you do. I have a better plan in mind.

Martha said, *"If only you had been here my brother would not have died." (John 11:21)* I know that like Martha, you have said "if only God had prevented that from happening!"

Never doubt in the dark what I have promised you in the light. Never doubt my character, or my promises, or my track record in your life ... I do care about you! It may look 'dead and buried' as far as you're concerned, but from where I stand, it's just a miracle in disguise ...

You're not alone today; I feel your pain, I know your heartache, and I can be touched by the feeling of your infirmities. Whatever stands between you and your answer, 'roll away the stone!' – get rid of it. Faith and unbelief don't mix!"

He added a promise "What I promised Martha, I promise you; *your brother will rise again." (John 11:23)*

Her tears fell at his feet; "Father, please forgive me. After the dragon had slain my brother, I felt that you were a weak King, a distant King who didn't care enough about us to prevent this from happening. I could not forgive you.

How could I follow you, and feel that way? Yet, I did. I followed you, because I had to. I got lost and you were the only way out of the wilderness. I had to follow you, even though I didn't really trust you."

Comforted, she looked up at him saying; "I forgive you. I don't understand how this could have happened, but I no longer need to know why. I will trust you. I now choose to follow you because I want to, not because I need to. Even if you treat me like Job, I'll still love you."

The Father brought her to her feet; "Listen Joanna, Job got back double. Come …." he said, as Joanna took his outstretched hand.

He led her outside, where a double rainbow hung against the dark gray sky.

Almond Grove

In the year 1999 the King awakened Joanna to a new day; "*Arise, my darling, my beautiful one, come with me. See! The winter is past; the rains are over and gone. Flowers appear on the earth; the season of singing has come; the cooing of doves is heard in our land. The fig tree forms its early fruit; the blossoming vines spread their fragrance. Arise, come, my darling; my beautiful one, come with me.*" Song of Songs 2:10-13 (NIV)

Dreaming, Joanna arose and walked slowly through the Kingdom, looking slowly about her. She found herself in a heavily forested area of hills, on a quiet country road that led to a lodge of sorts, which she never saw.

The road snaked back on itself in a big loop, and there were two small, rustic bridges over a stream, leading to a grove of trees.

There were trees of white blossom. They formed an avenue which she wandered dreamily through, admiring the beauty of the place.

Stirring in her sleep, she smiled. Before falling asleep the night before, she had asked the King for a clear direction of his will for her life, so she could know what to hope for. In order to meet the prince the King had promised, she had to believe he existed.

Joanna awakened, knowing the dream was significant. Out came the dream dictionary. Trees or shrubs in bloom meant a time of great prosperity and ease, both of body and of mind. She was pleased to hear it, but her question remained.

That night, as she was studying the King's scripture, he spoke to her of 'almond trees' and 'blossoms.' Taking her by the hand, the King led the Princess into his sanctuary, where a candlestick of pure gold with seven lamps burned in his presence. He had decorated the oil cups in the shape of almond blossoms. (Exodus 25:31)

"The word of the Lord came to me: 'what do you see, Jeremiah?' 'I see the branch of an almond tree' I replied. The Lord said to me, "you have seen correctly, for I am watching to see that my word is fulfilled"'
Jeremiah 1:11-12 (NIV)

"What do you see, Joanna?" the King asked.

"Almond trees?" she responded with a question.

He nodded.

"Lord, what are you trying to tell me?" she asked, looking through the dream dictionary. Dreaming of almond trees in bloom meant *to look forward with certainty to happiness in the married state.*

"Really?" she asked him, her eyes shining.

The King nodded; "In Hebrew, the word almond is very similar to the word 'watch'. You have seen correctly, for I am watching to see my word is fulfilled," he smiled, adding; "The almond tree is the first of the trees to awaken from its winter sleep."

Hope awakened like the almond blossom on a dead branch in winter. The King was granting her a second chance. This was his will and he was watching to see it fulfilled.

The next day he confirmed it when a friend who did not know of her dream mentioned they were going to plant an almond tree on their section.

"Really?" Joanna exclaimed, clapping her hands in delight.

Her friend was a bit taken aback at her enthusiasm.

"It's alright, there's a back story to this almond tree" she explained, as she smiled at the Lord, her eyes shining.

Millennium

Huddling down in her coat against the cold breeze blowing in from the Tasman Sea, Joanna kept a watchful eye on the three children in her care, who were laughing and skipping around the bonfire she built on the beach. They were having fun letting off fireworks to celebrate the eve of the Millennium.

Sighing, she watched the waves wash up on the black sand, wishing she could relax more, but she couldn't even drink. There were the children to look after, and she was on standby for the Y2K computer crisis.

Here she was at the turn of the century, the beginning of a new millennium, and she was feeling alone and friendless. It was too bad her best friend Nerida lived hundreds of kilometers away in Auckland.

Suddenly the fire exploded after her son Justin tossed a used firework into the flames. She jumped up to catch her daughter who'd rolled off the log they were sitting on.

The other two children ran backwards, shrieking and laughing. After the momentary excitement was over, it started to rain.

"That's it. Come on kids, it's time to go into town and join the street party," Joanna said, as she kicked sand onto the fire to put it out. In town, she joined some people she knew in the crowd milling around the Memorial Hall. It seemed the whole town counted the new millennium down as fireworks lit the sky, but her children were too tired to appreciate it.

Her first job for the year 2000 was to drop off her friend's child, and head home to get her own children to bed. The King watched her as she tucked them in, but she was too dispirited to reach for him.

Turning on the TV, she watched the celebrations begin in Sydney, the city that had welcomed her and been a place of refuge and healing. "Oh, why didn't I stay there?" she groaned, feeling depressed.

Her ex-husband had gone back there to live, breaking his promise to help her bring the children up.

She'd been unable to return because she was stuck bringing the kids up on her own, and lacked the money and resources to move.

The tears rolled down her face as she thought about what she'd lost leaving Sydney.

After their break-up, her ex-husband had casually told her that he'd expected her to go back to her dead-end job in the toxic little government department she'd been stuck in before leaving for Sydney. He didn't want her to resign without another job to go to, even though he could see how soul destroying the job was. It didn't matter; he wanted her pay.

How could she have gone back to a place where she was not respected, after she'd achieved so much in Sydney? It would be like an eagle waddling around with turkeys! She'd been shocked to realise how callous he was.

Either he'd never really cared about her, or she'd changed and he hadn't. She wished she'd known what he was thinking before being forced to leave Sydney.

Joanna reminded herself that things were different now. *She* was the one in control of her life, and would soon be returning to work in Australia.

She'd been seconded for four months work on an IT project at the same place as Prince Honest, White Flower's husband.

They'd moved to Canberra the year before. Joanna's children were going to live with their father and his new wife in Sydney for that four-month period.

Chapter Six

Looking around appreciatively at her new domain, Joanna gave a low whistle and smiled at White Flower as she checked out the rooms. "Oh wow, it has even got a spa bath!" she laughed. Her beautifully appointed Canberra apartment had every comfort and overlooked a heated salt water pool.

The only thing lacking was a view of Black Mountain and the Telstra Tower, which she got later when she moved up to the eighth floor. "Thank you; thank you, thank you," she said to the King, laughing with delight that this was going to be home for the next four months. The time foretold of in her dream, *a time of great prosperity and ease, both of body and of mind*, had come.

The work was easier than the work in New Zealand, although there was no sense of belonging on the teams. Her children joined her on the weekends, and they spent time with her old friends in Sydney and White Flower in Canberra. She also spent some of her leisure time sight-seeing with workmates.

In Canberra she found a vibrant church where she worshipped the King with the Australian believers. Mostly they were peaceful, happy days.

Although Joanna missed her children when she put them on the bus for Sydney at the end of the weekend, she made good use of her time alone.

"I will instruct you and teach you in the way you should go; I will guide you with my eye upon you" the King had promised Joanna.

He prompted her to take a Computer Servicing course at the Canberra Institute of Technology. It did not go down well with her employers, and she regretted mentioning it at work. They expected her to take a programming paper, which was the logical choice. Joanna resented their attitude. The course was attended in her own time, paid for with her own money and not work related.

She did not offer an explanation to them. Her rationale was that she wanted to explore a different area of Information Technology where she could learn about hardware as well as software.

Women did not occupy that arena, as she was soon to discover when she walked into a class full of men. Outside of her comfort zone at first, she soon felt at ease with her classmates.

"What are you going to get me into next?" she asked the King, as she strolled through the leafy campus to class. She breathed in the scent of the eucalypts, admired the blue and red Crimson Rosellas as they swooped through the trees, and thanked the Lord for the time to herself.

The small promise

Boom! "The sky is the limit," the announcer promised, as fireworks lit up the sky above Lake Burley Griffin. Music playing on massive speakers accompanied the pyrotechnics as Canberra celebrated Australia Day.

Joanna sat on the grass with a friend from work; her mind going back to the pits, where she'd promised the King that the sky was the limit. It was a big promise. She wished she could have told her friend about it, but he would not understand.

Her colleague disliked the King intensely and refused to have *anything* to do with the Kingdom, although he liked her! "You're one of *those* people, a 'God-botherer,' but you're alright," he'd often say.

It would have been great to meet a man she could share the experience with, a man who would *get it* when she talked about the King.

Her hope that she would meet a prince in Canberra was not to be.

"Father, why are you getting in my way?" she asked, scowling at the King as he separated her from a blonde prince at church. "Is there to be *no-one* here for me? If there is not *one single Prince* in your whole Kingdom for me, then I will forget about it, but I want to remain over here."

The King remained silent.

Autumn eventually came, turning Canberra red, green, and golden. In the early mornings a thick fog often rolled in, throwing a white blanket over the land.

Her future seemed to be shrouded in the same fog. It was time to return to life in small town New Zealand.

She wanted to stay in Australia, but the doors were closed to her. Her ex-husband and his wife, who'd been her former friend, did not want to extend the children's stay beyond the four-month period. In fact, his wife believed Joanna should have "thanked them" for looking after "her children." And the job she arranged in Canberra dissolved.

"I don't want to go back to New Zealand! Please don't make me go back there," she cried, trying the closed doors.

She needed a job and caregiver for the children before she could stay in Australia.

"Father, are you to say *nothing?* I hate it back in New Zealand. You know I *never* chose to live there. You know that! How can the sky be the limit in the small town of a small country that I despise?"

"Who despises the day of small things?" the King asked, quoting from Zechariah 4:10. *"Do not despise these small beginnings,"* he added; "for I the Lord rejoice to see the work begin. I've already

determined what I want to build in your life, and I am laying your foundations accordingly. Do not expect it to be easy."

She started to cry. "I don't want to build my life back in New Zealand. There is *nothing* for me there!"

"It is better that you return," he comforted her; "Stay and raise the children there, even if for you it is the day of small things. You are to remain, pull the plough, and *mind my household.* Sometimes the Kingdom is about slaying dragons, and sometimes it's the day of small things. I know it's not interesting, but it's necessary. Go back and keep building, brick by brick, day by day and stone by stone. Restore the ruined house, even if it is only you left to do the work.

Blessed is the servant who I find minding my house when I return."
The King finished with a small promise, "Do not worry about your property while you are over here, for I am keeping watch …"
"You shall know that your tent is in peace, you shall visit your dwelling and find nothing amiss."
Job 5:24 (NKJ)

The Doldrums

Returning to the place of 'same old, same old', Joanna numbly unpacked; stuffing her feelings away in the wardrobe with her clothes.

White Flower and Prince Honest had stayed at her place with their children on a trip back to New Zealand during her absence. Her home had been lovingly tended by White Flower, who made it welcoming and clean for her return, leaving little gifts for her to find.

The only thing that had gone wrong was in the little Princess's room. "Mum!" she heard her daughter Nicole scream at the discovery her new Ken doll had been decapitated by one of White Flower's children. Trying to stick Ken's head back on, Joanna stifled a grin, thinking of males with their heads ripped off. She wasn't a female praying-mantis.

Her workmates all thought she was a man-hater, because she'd shown no interest in her male colleagues in the three years she'd been there. That went to show how little they knew her.

She couldn't very well say "My prince will come; I'm waiting for the man God has promised."

Joanna tried to get to a more positive state of mind. At least she had friends now; and Deborah and other good people welcomed her back. But as the days passed Joanna found she was having trouble fitting back into her old life.

Her disappointment at being back coloured everything. Listless and depressed, she was going through a dry place with the King. Her life lacked direction. At times her Bible acted as a map, but when she tried to consult the map, she couldn't find the road. She felt disoriented and lost.

The old routine wasn't working. On Sundays she kept going to church once a week to teach the children, but her feet were dragging. It was a far cry from the vibrant atmosphere of the King's gathering at Canberra. They were often late, running along the street to make it through the door just before the minister.

"I don't fit in there" she complained to Deborah.

"You need to find a different church. What do they ever do for you?" Deborah growled, exasperated at her lack of action.

While Joanna mulled over where to worship the King, she got the internet. It ended her isolation, at least virtually as the world opened up to her. The connection with the wider world awoke a conviction that the man God had chosen was not from her country.

When she was younger the King had talked about her marrying an American. A distant cousin had the same idea and believed the promise for herself. Joanna dismissed it as fanciful thinking. Her parents often said "she had a big imagination." The years buried the idea, but now it was back.

What if it was not just a fanciful idea; what if the man the King had chosen really was from the States? *"If* the chosen man is American, can you find me friends on the internet from his part of the States?" Joanna asked the King.

Her request was granted, and a sign called 'Florida' appeared. The friends she met through email were all met by chance, and were all from Florida. They came from far off places named Jacksonville, Fort Lauderdale, and Kissimmee.

Jim, her friend from Kissimmee nicknamed it 'Kismet', the word his spell checker changed it to. It meant fate or destiny.

Along with the sign of Florida came her first computer repair job. She fixed Jim's computer in Kissimmee using the training she received from the Canberra Institute of Technology.

Florida was an interesting sign, but her logical mind dismissed it. Florida was over 11,000 kilometers away. It was an idea best kept in the realms of fantasy.

She took a dim view of using the internet to try and find the American, but she did use it for study and for information.

The King was mostly ignored while she explored the web, escaping the constrictions of life in small town New Zealand.

"You need to pay attention to me and change direction" the King warned, showing her a picture of a wind-surfer who kept falling over in the water because she wasn't catching the wind.

He said; *"Your rigging hangs loose: the mast is not held secure; the sail is not spread." Isaiah 33:23 (NIV)*

The Valley of Baca

Weeping Joanna entered the dry valley of Baca. She came stumbling into the King's presence, holding her latest performance review. Normally her reviews were good, but this one was just wrong. "Watch your back" someone at work had warned her upon her return from Canberra. He'd been right.

"Oh, Father" she sobbed as she told him of her troubles at work. "It is so unjust".

At first the King seemed a long way off. She drew near enough to hear him speak the word 'Ecclesiastes.' Thumbing through the Bible, the only words that spoke to her were these;

"If the axe is dull and its edge unsharpened; more strength is needed, but skill will bring success." Ecclesiastes 10:10 (NIV)

"I need skill, not strength! These people have better skills, because they got better training, and they're more experienced. I haven't been there for twenty years like they have. This is *not* a level playing field. I am working with all of my strength to compensate. If skill will bring success, then help me develop it," she pleaded.

"Don't fear them!" the King replied, adding "It is I, even I, who comforts you. Who are you to fear their reproach? At the outset, you did not stand up to the bullies and the culture when you needed to. You must believe in yourself, otherwise the dragons in the workplace will always try to undermine you."

The King saw her pick up on the word *dragon*.

"No, this is not an attack by the dragon, at least not directly. It is about your character.

I have allowed this struggle and bad time to befall you, for their bad performance review will not matter down the road, but mine does. The one I will give on the day you stand before me is the judgment you should worry about, and there are things I am not pleased with."

She drew a ragged breath, thinking things had been wrong for a long time, and had gotten even worse since she had returned from Canberra, especially at work.

To add to her misery, she found out that Silver-tongue had joined the same company, in a different division down in Wellington.

Feeling like she was being stalked she nervously looked over her shoulder every time she worked in Wellington, careful that their paths did not cross. She did not talk about him to anyone at work.

How could he get into such a high position in the company when she'd proven her technical skills were superior to his? He knew it and she knew it.

"What fault do you find in me?" she asked, fixing her eyes on the King.

"You've been walking in your *own* strength" he replied.

"*My strength?*" she asked incredulously, "If the axe is dull, and I don't have the tools to sharpen it, then strength is the only thing I have! Forgive me for asking, but *how is that bad?*"

"I know you've had to be self-reliant, but it's no good when you can't trust others. I've heard you say "I'll do it myself" rather than ask for help from someone you don't trust.

You need to learn to rely on me;

"I will lead you in righteousness, which produces quietness and confidence; and the work of righteousness shall be peace; and the effect of righteousness quietness and assurance forever."" Isaiah 32:16-17 (NKJ)

Tears stung her eyes. The words were a comfort but the King's words goaded her.

Joanna wanted quietness, confidence and self-assurance. The time had come when she accepted that she would have to unlearn everything she'd been taught, even the 'good things.'

"To be strong, I must rely on you and others?" she asked.

"Yes. Look to me for your strength," he replied, giving her a word from Matthew 11:29, *"Come to me, all you who are weary and burdened, and I will give you rest. Take my yoke, and learn of me, for I am gentle and humble in heart and you will find rest for your soul."*

"I know for you it is a place of wounding," he added, "and you will feel you are putting yourself in harm's way - but I am here, and I am here in your circle of friends. I brought them to you and I will bring others like them who you can trust."

"I'm at the end of myself," she sighed; "You lead, and I'll follow. I know that *you* would not give me the workplace bully as a mentor, or demand that I seek help from those who use and abuse me. If you are in charge, then I am ready to trust those whom *you* bring me."

The King's reply was a promise; *"In repentance and rest is your salvation. In quietness and trust is your strength." Isaiah 30:15 (NIV)*

Picking up her staff, she resumed her long and lonely journey through the valley of Baca.

To lift her spirits, she sang a song;

"How happy are those whose strength comes from you, who are eager to make the pilgrimage to Mount Zion. As they pass through the dry valley of Baca, it becomes a place of springs.

The autumn rain fills it with pools; they grow stronger as they go. They will see the King of Kings on Zion." Psalm 84:5-7 (GNT)

Ishmael

"Would I bring you a stone if you asked for Bread?" the King kept asking Joanna, wanting her to have more faith in him. *"Or would I bring you a snake if you asked for fish?"* he added;

"If you know how to give good gifts to your children, how much more will I give to you, if you ask?" (Matthew 7:9)

Used to fighting for everything she wanted, Joanna was reluctant to ask the King to provide. She was afraid of being disappointed.

Knowing that she needed to trust in the King more, she began by relaxing her grip on money and spending a bit extra on the household. One of her purchases was a fridge she bought from Ishmael, a friend at work. It was nearly new, but when she opened the door, she found he hadn't cleaned it.

The next day Joanna eyed Ishmael, who sat at the desk facing hers. Although she called him by a different name, the name the King gave him was *Ishmael*, meaning "whom God hears."

Ishmael had escaped Iraq, which was still in the ruthless grip of the dictator Saddam Hussein.

Ishmael was a moderate Moslem, not the hairy fundamentalist type with the waving finger. A gentle charming man with a ready laugh, he was popular at work, even with the bullies. For Joanna, he was a friendly face in the office.

She often teased him in a gentle manner. On this day her eyes caught and held his, as she said *"You* have a fridge to clean!" Ishmael gave her a guilty smile.

After work her mentor Livia arrived and the fridge was forgotten as they discussed the King.

"The King says he wants to give me good things, but I get a negative feeling when I hear it. How can I get past this?" Joanna asked, while cooking dinner.

Just then Ishmael arrived unexpectedly. Breaking off her conversation, she introduced him. Livia left, raising her eyebrows at Ishmael's presence.

Shaking her head at her mentor's presumption, Joanna looked at Ishmael.

She supposed he was handsome but she'd never looked at him that way. And she didn't want to start now.

This was not a man she could be interested in. They were from different kingdoms, different cultures, different backgrounds, and different faiths. And he was married, even though he'd been living alone for the last six months.

His wife had left for Australia and refused to come back to New Zealand. She couldn't blame her for that.

Joanna had been encouraging him to go and join his wife and children in Australia. Meanwhile Ishmael had been trying to get her to visit, but she'd ignored him.

"I hope you like good old English cooking. You're lucky we're not having pork," she teased as he joined them at the table.

He hadn't been invited for dinner, but since he'd arrived at mealtime, she'd added a plate of food for him.

Ishmael smiled and pointed at the sign on the wall called 'Mum's rules', which said *"I have made it, and you will eat it, and you will like it."*

"I would eat it," he promised.

"Then you're a bad Moslem!" she joked.

After the children were put to bed, she made Ishmael help with the dishes. It soon became obvious that he'd never cleaned a dish in his life.

As they were laughing about the suds going everywhere, he suddenly lifted his arms out of the sink and soundly kissed her. Taken by surprise, Joanna allowed the kiss, which she found to be very agreeable. Tightening his arms around her, Ishmael confessed he'd grown to love her.

"What? When did *that* happen?" she asked, confused and blindsided, her head reeling.

Ishmael told Joanna of all the good he found in her and the day he'd fallen in love.

"I don't believe you!" she exclaimed, retreating into denial. How could it be?

"It's true. I went to Canberra for you!" he insisted.

Her mind flashed back to Canberra. It would have been a wasted trip for him, as she had not paid him much attention. Joanna simply thought he'd come over to Canberra for a holiday, to stay with other people on her team.

On his arrival in Australia, she remembered asking him to come down from Sydney on the Friday night bus with her children.

After greeting him at the bus station he'd paid her a compliment; saying she looked beautiful.

All Joanna thought was that he was being polite. After greeting him happily she'd immediately switched her attention to her children. He'd been in her peripheral vision after that.

The pieces of the puzzle were rapidly assembled in her mind. How had she not seen this! How could she have been so blind? Now she was fighting a fire that Ishmael had lit, smothering unwanted and uninvited flames of desire. This was no fire to warm herself by.

The dishes and the fridge were forgotten as her body threatened to turn traitor. Although Ishmael held her close, she willed herself not to give in to him.

The King's words kept her in check; *"Flee from sexual immorality. Every other sin a person commits is outside the body, but the sexually immoral person sins against his own body." (1 Corinthians 6:18)*

She was supposed to run from temptation – but she was at home and her children were sleeping, so the King heard some frantic prayers instead.

Eventually she was able to make him go home.

Exhaling, she went back to the pile of dishes in the kitchen.

"What was THAT all about?" she asked the King, tired and shaken; "Where did that come from? Have I ever flirted with him, or encouraged him?" The question was directed as much at herself, as him. Then anger came, replacing astonishment. "This really sucks. He is leaving for Australia where he'll go back to his wife, and he wants me too! How could he do this to me? He's just like all the rest," she added sourly, wanting to despise him.

"Listen, he means no harm to you," the King replied. "He is vulnerable and thinking only of himself. He wanted to know where he stood with you before deciding to return to his wife."

"Like a bird that strays from its nest; is a man who is away from his home" he added, quoting a proverb from Proverbs 27:8.

"Unbelievable" Joanna remarked, frowning and shaking her head. "He said he *was* home, as he took me in his arms!" she added, pushing down unwanted feelings.

"He is drawn to me and the Kingdom within," the King replied; "But he is very wrong to think I would allow this. This is not his nest. Stay away from him," he warned.

"You don't need to tell me that!" she retorted.

After that, Joanna kept her distance from Ishmael. It was weird at work, they were very attracted to one another, yet no-one noticed the changed and charged atmosphere between them.

"Run!" the King said at the end of each day, and she bolted for home.

"He needs to go to Australia, NOW" Joanna warned.

The King got him a job and an airline ticket in a matter of days.

Ishmael's last night in New Zealand came. Joanna relented and allowed him to come over to say goodbye. She did not know how she felt about him. Their spirits recognised each other.

She had always felt a bond with him as they were both children of Abraham. He was a true son of Ishmael, whereas she was adopted into the line of Isaac. He respected the King as a prophet, but had never heard of salvation.

They discussed having a relationship. If she allowed him to stay, Ishmael would not get on the plane. "I need to marry a Christian" Joanna told him. God became the issue. Ishmael could not see what the problem was. He respected Jesus as a prophet. In spite of believing her book the Bible had been changed, he believed they worshiped the same God.

He thought their spiritual descent from Abraham and united belief in God would be enough.

She knew it wouldn't;

For I can testify about them that they are zealous for God, but their zeal is not based on knowledge. Since they did not know the righteousness that comes from God and sought to establish their own, they did not submit to God's righteousness. Christ is the end of the law so that there may be righteousness for everyone who believes.

The righteousness that is by faith says: "The word is near you; it is in your mouth and in your heart; that is, the word of faith we are proclaiming: **That if you confess with your mouth, 'Jesus is Lord' and believe in your heart that God raised him from the dead, you will be saved."** *Romans 10:5-9 (NIV)*

Although Ishmael revered his god, he could not understand how Joanna could hear from her God. Joanna knew his god didn't speak because he was a lifeless idol.

She did her best to explain what Ishmael as a Moslem had not been taught - his need for salvation.

Even though he could not be hers, she wanted him for the King, who she wished he would someday believe in. Every time the word 'love' came up she had a problem.

He was very attractive but she guarded her heart and kept herself safe. From experience Joanna knew that discipline weighed an ounce but regret weighed a ton. Exercising self-control she said 'no' to Ishmael.

Joanna had to admit that Ishmael made her feel good about herself as a woman. In the valley of Baca, this was an oasis. Her weary soul had found solace in his words and his arms.

"You are like water for me in a desert," she told Ishmael. For just a little while, she no longer felt alone.

"Oh God, go with him," she asked, watching him leave in the winter's dawn; "Forgive us for our weakness for each other. May he come to know what you did for him on the cross, and put his trust in you."

The River

The King was displeased with Joanna.
"Why go to Assyria to drink water from the river?" he questioned with an edge to his voice.
"What?" Joanna asked, puzzled.
"I heard you tell Ishmael he was like water for you in the desert," he growled jealously.
Speaking from Jeremiah 2 he said;
"I remember the devotion of your youth, how as a bride you loved me and followed me through the desert, through a land not sown. Long ago you broke off your yoke and tore off your bonds; you said 'I will not serve you!'
He paused.
"What fault did your ancestors find in me, that they strayed so far from me?" he asked.
"You of this generation," he continued, *"consider the word of the Lord: Have I been a desert to you? Or a land of great darkness? Why do my people say 'we are free to roam; we will come to you no more?'*
Does a maiden forget her jewellery? Or a bride her wedding ornaments? Yet my people have forgotten me, days without number!
My people have committed two sins: They have forsaken me, the spring of living water, and have dug their own cisterns, broken cisterns that cannot hold water."

"Now why go to Assyria to drink water from the river?" the King repeated his question.

Worried, Joanna went to get the atlas.

"I'll bet Iraq, where Ishmael comes from, was once part of Assyria!" she muttered.

She was right. The King wanted to know why she'd gone to Iraq to satisfy her thirst. Or why she'd gone to Babylon. No doubt 'the river' was the river of Babylon. When the King spoke of 'the river' he meant 'the spirit'.

He was waiting.

Grimacing, Joanna decided to be honest; "Yes, I admit it. I did forsake you for men ... and there is a risk I still might. You do not have arms that you can wrap around me or a body that can comfort me. I can't even *see* you.

First of all, you wanted to be my father, and that was bad enough after I thought you let my brother die - but now you're sounding like a jealous lover! So, I do prefer men to you. I admit it!

To love you means denying myself! I understand that - and for the last four years I've tried to please you by being on my own. But I can't live like this anymore! What can I do? What more do you want of me?"

"Why don't you trust me? Have you forgotten my promises so quickly?" the King asked in anger and sadness. "I seek your highest best! *You* are the one who chose the desert, and that is why Ishmael appeared!"

"I'm sorry" Joanna replied, tearfully. "Help me to want you *more*" she asked as she bowed before him.

His purpose

Puzzled, Joanna wondered why this foreign man had come into her life. Ishmael was not part of the King's will, she knew that - but what *was* the King's purpose?

She remembered a word the King had given her a few years before meeting Ishmael;

"I say my purpose will stand and I will do all that I please. From the east I summon a bird of prey; from a far-off land, a man to fulfill my purpose. What I have said, I will bring about; what I have planned, that will I do." Isaiah 46:10-11

It seemed the Lord had planned this, but why?

"Why did you bring this eastern man from a far-off land into my life?" she asked, confused.

"You asked for him" the King answered.

"When did I do that?" she asked.

"You asked me to bring you a man who sees you for who you really are and who desires you," he reminded her; "And I said, be careful of what you ask!"

"Good grief!" she exclaimed, surprised; "Well you didn't have to answer *that* prayer!"

"It wasn't a prayer – it was a wish" he corrected her.

"Wish or prayer, whatever it was, you allowed the temptation," she stated.

"I made sure he wasn't there for long," he replied;

"No temptation has seized you except what is common to man, and I am faithful; I will not let you be tempted beyond what you

can bear. But when you are tempted, I will also provide a way out so that you can stand up under it." (1 Corinthians 10:13)
"I'm going to have to watch what I ask you for in future!" she said, shaking her head.

Joanna now understood a promise the Lord made when she was working on her boundaries;

"The day for rebuilding your walls will come, the day for extending your boundaries. In that day people will come to you, from Assyria and the cities of Egypt, even from Egypt to Euphrates, and from sea to sea, and from mountain to mountain." Micah 7:11-12 (NIV)

The King forgave Joanna for what she'd said to Ishmael. She'd given him an honest response and she'd kept faith with him. Her boundaries had been tested and they stood. He often used Ishmael as a test; and Ishmael as a type always had to appear first.

The wedding ring

"I hate this," Joanna said, looking at the King sadly. She missed Ishmael, even though it was a go nowhere romance.

"I can't have him by my side, because he's already married and he's not from this Kingdom. He belongs to that war mongering prophet who cared nothing for women and had all those wives, the youngest of who was only nine. You had no one, because you gave yourself for us, to save us. If only he could *see* the *difference* between you."

Believing she'd been put in Ishmael's life to be a friend and ambassador for the King, she'd done everything for him she could - but instead of wanting the King, he had turned around and wanted *her,* the servant.

If only she could dismiss him as a liar and an unfaithful person, and walk away without a backward glance. But he'd been her friend. She did not want to go there.

If she could not hate him then the only other choice was to feel something for him. It reminded her of the affair that Silver-tongue had lied and manipulated her into.

"Oh, why did he have to act like that, act like Silver-tongue?" she groaned.

She was sick of struggling through each day on her own – coping with the emptiness, the loneliness, the unwanted advances from men and the children being fatherless.

There were no male relatives on her side and her son Justin had grown nearly as tall has her. Although she made sure her children spent as much time as they could with their father's parents, her son needed someone besides his grandfather when his father was not around.

She had to remind herself of what the King had said about Ishmael. He had acted selfishly, but he hadn't plotted against her like Silver-tongue. One thing she was glad of; the regard she'd seen in Ishmael's eyes. He esteemed her. In her heart she treasured it. Love was love, even if it wasn't from the right man. But it was the wrong kind of love. The right kind warmed like a fire in the hearth, the wrong kind raged out of control, burning homes and lives down.

At work she looked at Ishmael's empty desk and although she missed him, she realised it was the King she wanted. She'd come to realise that men and women often looked to each other to fulfill a need that only God could truly meet, and human relationships were not a substitute.

"It is you I want, you!" she called out to the King loudly and powerfully in her mind; "It has to be you. I choose you, not Ishmael."

As soon as she could, she ran into the Kingdom, seeking the King. Finding him in the desert, she bowed low saying "Jesus, Lord. I thirst. I thirst for *you*."

Happy he'd been chosen over a man at last; the Lord drew near and spoke from Hosea 2:14-15; *"Therefore I am now going to allure you; I will lead you into the desert, and speak tenderly to you. There I will give back your vineyards, and I will make the valley of Achor, the valley of trouble a door of hope. Then you will respond as in the days of your youth, as in the day you came up out of Egypt. 'In that day', declares the Lord, you will call me 'my husband'; you will no longer call me 'my master.'"*

Not long after that, two rings were found on the chair in front of the fireplace. One was a gold wedding band, the other a smaller ring with a diamond chip. Putting them away, she asked everyone who'd visited the house if they'd lost the rings. No-one came forward for them and the gold band became hers.

She kept the smaller diamond ring for her daughter to wear when she was older. It was a mystery where the rings had come from. She held the gold band in her hand and studied it. It fitted her third finger perfectly.

She spoke to the King. "Lord, this jewellery is a puzzle to us, for the rings seem to have appeared out of nowhere. Did you give these rings to us?"

The King nodded, saying "Now we are on the same page, read further."

She read the next lines of Hosea;

"I will betroth you to me forever; Yes, I will betroth you to me in righteousness and justice, in loving kindness and mercy; I will betroth you to me in faithfulness, and you shall know the LORD." Hosea 2:19 (NKJ)

Wellspring

Groaning, Joanna put her head in her hands. The Lord wanted her to tell the workplace chaplain about Ishmael. "Oh no, God, no" she said, appalled. How embarrassing. Afraid, she made a silent deal with him; "Alright. If he comes out of that office *right now* and heads over to my desk, I'll talk to him ..."

Immediately the King fetched him.

"Oh, God," she groaned again, but kept her side of the bargain.

The chaplain was a good man and she trusted him.

"I must speak to you privately about something," she said. Meeting him in her own time outside of the office, she told him what had happened. Robert listened carefully and they prayed about the matter. She felt she was in a safe place; and experienced a sense of relief at being heard.

He called to mind a poem *"There's A Hole in My Sidewalk"* by Portia Nelson, where a person had trouble with a deep hole in a sidewalk.

The first time they fell in it wasn't their fault, the second time it was, the third time it was a habit, the fourth time they skirt around it, and the fifth time they choose another road.

"Where are you on this journey?" he asked.

"Ah, somewhere between hole number three and four," she replied ruefully.

"It could have been worse," he reassured her, "You stumbled, but you didn't fall."

"Why has this happened to me again though?" she asked.

"It may be God trying to show you something. I can hand you over to my wife for counsel. She will help you find the road without the potholes. Would you like that?" he answered.

She nodded and he introduced her to his wife princess Linda, who was running a course in the year of 2001 called 'Search for Significance'. It was a safe place which was helping and equipping a small group of women who needed to trust God as a Father.

Knowing the road at Linda's group led back to him, the Father said;

"My people will return weeping, praying as I lead them back. I will guide them to streams of water, on a smooth road where they will not stumble." (GNT)

They were taught about the Father heart of God. In the beginning men and women were created in his image to be his family, but after the Fall they became estranged from him and were disinherited. It got worse with each generation. Instead of God being the Father he became a judge.

In his attempt to be reconciled he sent his only son the King to come into the fallen world to save them.

It helped Joanna understand why she mattered to God the Father. She learned how great the value of every human life was to God - and with that knowledge came self-worth.

The road back had signs for Joanna to follow. She sighed with relief. For a long time, she'd been travelling without seeing anything.

One night, led by Princess Linda, they came to a desert well at Samaria, where they found the King talking to a Samaritan woman. It was a dry place. When he asked the woman for water she replied, *"Sir, the well is deep and there is no cup."*

He taught her about living water, saying *"whoever drinks the water I give will never thirst. Indeed, the water I give will become a spring of water welling up to eternal life."*

When the woman asked for the living water, he dealt with the issue of her five husbands and the man she was currently living with, without tearing her down. (John 4:7-18)

Joanna understood where they were going with the teaching. The King had already taken her there after her encounter in the desert with Ishmael.

"With joy you will draw water from the wells of salvation," he'd promised after she'd repented of finding Ishmael's attention refreshing.
The well at Samaria was called Jacob's well.
Joanna smiled. She was at the first well, and the King had given her a place to head for on her map!

"Where is the well of salvation?" Joanna asked.
Linda groaned, thinking she'd gone off on a tangent.

Realising she'd been given a private revelation, Joanna went back to knowledge to show she understood what was being taught;
"I can see that the Samaritan woman wasn't sure what the living water was, but she wanted what Jesus offered. She lived in a desert, she walked alone and she no longer wanted to keep coming back to Jacob's well - a place where she was not welcome, to draw water. I know that like her, only God can meet our thirst."

"Where do I find this well?" Joanna asked when she was alone with the King.
Taking her into the desert, he pointed at the stars.
"I am the living water," he declared, giving her the sign of Aquarius, the water bearer.

Speaking from Psalm 147 he said; *"I determined the number of stars and called each of them by name."* His finger stopped at the constellation of the water bearer and pourer, Aquarius. The star Saad al Melik, the record of the pouring forth, shone brightly from the right shoulder. "It is I of who Aquarius speaks."

Her eyes strayed from the stars back to the King. The desert behind him seemed as endless as the stars.

She said "You know the way to the desert wells. Don't let my life ebb away here. Lead me through the desert, to a city where I can settle. I am going to follow you, follow you all the way home ... wherever home is."

The King read from Psalm 107: 7-8;
"Some wandered in the trackless desert wastelands, finding no way to a city where they could settle. They were hungry and thirsty, and their lives ebbed away. Then they cried out to the Lord in their trouble, and I delivered them from their distress. I led them by a straight way to a city where they could settle."

He added; "Study my word and *stay with me.* Do not stop in the desert where there is no water, or lose heart. I will bring you home."

Livia was not impressed. When Joanna tried to show Livia how the signs of the constellations spoke of the King, she warned Joanna about astrology, and told her not to get interested in *'that stuff.'*

Joanna replied; "Listen, I follow what I read in the Bible. I'm not going to heed astrologers, or go off reading horoscopes - but I can see these are signs that speak of the King! These signs seem to be the remnants of a great story of salvation in the stars, but it has been corrupted and fallen into ruin.

'The heavens declare the glory of God; the skies proclaim the work of his hands. Day after day they pour forth speech; night after night they reveal knowledge. They have no speech; they use no words; no sound is heard from them. Yet their voice goes out into all the earth, their words to the ends of the world.'" Psalm 19:1-6 (NIV)

After Livia left, Joanna spoke to the King;
"I really respect Livia, but on this we will just have to disagree. I know you would not give me the sign of Aquarius if it would lead me astray."

Chapter Seven

One day in the autumn of 2002 a dark shadow fell across her path. It was Silver-tongue, stalking her from the shadows. Joanna had given him a narcissistic injury he had not recovered from. Angry that she'd rejected him, he lived for the day when he would get even. Lusting for control, he maneuvered himself to get back into her life.

Aware of Silver-tongue's plans, the King led Joanna further into the wilderness. The dry valley of Baca led to the valley of Achor through a rocky gorge full of shadow. The name 'Achor' meant trouble. Speaking to her tenderly from Hosea, he promised he would make the Valley of Achor a door of hope.

Joanna didn't know there was trouble ahead. After four years of full-time work, she'd finally earned enough money to afford a decent holiday. They discussed where they should go over dinner. Her son Justin suggested they go to see Marjorie, her lifelong friend who she'd found at the age of ten after putting a letter in an apple crate.

Her letter turned up at Marjorie and her husband Roger's greengrocer's shop in the Isle of Wight.

A kind woman, Marjorie took the time to write to the child; and with every letter Joanna felt she was important and special, and mattered. In turn she loved Marjorie like a grandmother, as did her children. They'd traveled to visit each other, Joanna once and Marjorie twice.

Joanna was surprised at the children's choice; she'd expected them to suggest the fun parks of Surfers Paradise in Australia. She thought it was a great idea, but the cost and the distance were prohibitive. Marjorie lived at the other end of the earth.

While saying grace she addressed the King with this practical need; "Lord, we want to go and see Marjorie, but you know how far it is. I've got enough money for Australia, but not England. Can we please have the money and the time for the trip?"

It was a dangerous prayer. The Lord answered by getting rid of her job! In a way, it was no loss. She didn't want to be there anyway. Even so, she'd lost her place in her chosen field as far as her career went.

She faced an uncertain future without a job or a husband, and there was a ten-week period without pay to get through.

The King told her to spend the redundancy money on the trip to England. "You've got the time, and you've got the money," he pointed out.

Joanna looked at him, eyebrows raised at the way he'd answered her prayer.

"I get into trouble asking you for things!" she remarked.

"Don't worry," he reassured her, "I've got this. It's all part of my plan. It was time to leave. You'll find out *why* soon enough."

Down in Wellington, Silver-tongue gloated about leading the testing team at the multinational company Joanna had just been made redundant from. But he was disappointed that he would not be 'managing her.' That's what he'd wanted the most.

Pompous, self-important and clearly still obsessed, it hadn't occurred to him that she would have resigned first.

The next day he rang Joanna. It was the first time he'd spoken to her in years.

Joanna's lip curled with revulsion at hearing his voice, but she let him talk. Why did he phone her? Delusional, he bragged that he'd been appointed to lead one of the teams she'd been part of. Understanding dawned on Joanna's face. So, *this* was why she was out of the company!

The flattery started as soon as she said she forgave him. Unable to see the disgust on her face Silver-tongue thought he was back in with a chance. The flattering words didn't have any effect on her. Forgiveness did not mean she liked him, or wanted to rekindle the 'relationship.' She'd learned that if she forgave the abusers, it would be the last she'd see of them.

After speaking to him all she wanted to do was vomit and have a bath.

Hanging up with a look of distaste, her face brightened when she saw the King.

"Now I know why I'm not there anymore!" she told him; "You got me out of that place in the nick of time, and with a lump sum payout. Nice! Thank you so much for the redundancy. Now I have enough money to visit Marjorie."

Joanna moved on leaving Narcissus staring into a pool, captured and captivated by his own reflection.
Narcissists suffered from excessive, overweening pride; gazing at themselves in admiration, all the time hiding from their true selves.
The unfortunate women and men who loved them were merely objects, a dumping ground. They projected all their faults and character flaws onto their victims, stealing their virtues in return. She, who had been no exception to having her identity robbed in this manner, said;
"May it be your own face that you see reflected in the water and may it be your own self that you see in your heart." (Proverbs 27:19)

"I don't hate him anymore," Joanna told the Lord; "I feel nothing for him but pity and contempt, and I see nothing in him but an empty shell. How can he repent if he can't see himself as he really is?"

"Now you see why I hate pride," the Lord replied with sorrow.

"Was he stalking me again?" she asked, not wanting to always have to look over her shoulder.

"This is the last time you will find him lurking in the shadows," the King promised; "He will *never* be in a position of authority over you, nor bother you ever again."

"Good" she said with relief.

Now she could truly move on.

He added, "I know why authority is another word you distrust, but don't let him poison the well. I will teach you about true authority, when you are ready."

The Door of Hope, and the third wish

Sighing, Joanna rolled her eyes and crossed her arms as she listened to the Sunday sermon.
"This is going to be a lecture on how wives should obey - all for the man's benefit!" she thought cynically.
She was sitting at the entrance to the Door of Hope - not that she knew it. The door was well hidden.

That day the message was about Kingdom authority.
"What is the spirit of Christ?" Iliafi the apostle began; "It is the spirit of submission. In marriage, it is for the man to lay down his life for the woman."

What? Joanna sat up, startled. That got her attention. She listened intently, hearing that marriages in the Kingdom were meant for the man to put his wife *first;* that the husband would sacrifice for the wife.

In her world, it had always been the other way around. Her grandmother had sacrificed her hopes and dreams for her blind husband. Her mother had been looked down on by her father and expected to follow his lead.

Joanna had lived her whole life thinking she had to lay down her life for the man – and she'd sacrificed everything for her first husband.

Wary of being trapped, she didn't want to be in a situation where she'd have to go through that again. Had she believed a lie? Her belief that she had to die to self for a man was holding her back from wanting a second marriage. She'd had enough loss in her life.

"She will naturally submit to any man when the love is there, and call her husband 'Lord,'" Iliafi preached. Joanna hated the word 'submit', but in this instance she agreed wholeheartedly. This was a game changer.

Iliafi read from the Bible;
"Husbands, love your wives just as Christ loved the Church and gave himself up for her to make her holy, cleansing her by the washing with water through the word, and to present her to himself as a radiant church, without stain or wrinkle or any other blemish, but holy and blameless.
In this same way, husbands ought to love their wives as their own bodies. He who loves his wife loves himself."
Ephesians 5:22-28 (NIV)

Recognising the truth, Joanna changed her mind about marriage. The Lord had given her a key to a better place; a future she never dared hope for.

The key unlocked the Door of Hope.

Stepping through the door she walked into a fragrant garden. Everything appeared in a different light. Living water flowed through a fountain. Engraved on the rock behind it was a word from Proverbs 13:14, *"The teaching of the wise is a fountain of life."*

The daughter of the King emerged, approaching the Father with her eyes shining.

"Is this what you want for me?" Joanna asked.

The King nodded.

"Really?" she asked, smiling.

He nodded again.

"You want a husband who will lay down his life for me, just as you did for us?" she asked again, to be sure.

The King nodded for the third time.
"How do you feel about the word submission now?" he asked.

"I no longer feel it's a bad word," she allowed.

"How would you feel about a man who submits to me under that covenant?" he asked.
"I would feel safe with him," she answered.

"Would you respect a man who would love you enough to die for you?" he asked.

"Yes" she agreed happily.

Joanna was a changed woman. Strengthened in her faith, she hoped for something better from that day forward, although she still thought of Ishmael.

"Father, instead of putting in front of me a man I cannot have, please put in front of me a man I *can* have," she asked while sitting on her porch.

The King was happy. He could do something with this, her third wish. Until then, held back by wrong ideas about submission, her last two wishes had nothing to do with marriage.
He had fulfilled those wishes, to teach her a lesson each time. It might seem harsh, but he was treating her like a daughter.

When he'd done it, he spoke from Proverbs 3:12; *"My children, do not despise the Lord's discipline, and do not resent his rebuke, because the Lord disciplines those he loves, as a father the child he delights in."*

"I hear you. Who do you have in mind?" he asked.

"You choose" she replied, remembering his promises about the chosen man.

A new thing

Looking around her, Joanna could see the desert was changing. She was headed for a little river lined with willows that flowed in front of a mountain pass. It looked like a place where she could rest.
As the King led, he said;
"See, I am doing a new thing! Now it springs up; do you not perceive it? I am making a way in the wilderness and streams in the wasteland." Isaiah 43:20

"Is there anything I need to do while overseas?" she asked.

"Rest," the King replied; "I want you to relax and have a good time."

What a difference he made as her acting husband. He accompanied them to the ends of the earth and took good care of them.
"He tends his flock like a shepherd: He gathers the lambs in his arms and carries them close to his heart; he gently leads the mothers." (Isaiah 40:11)

It was like coming home as the ferry sailed across the Solent from Southampton. The last time Joanna had been at Marjorie's she'd been twenty. The first thing they did was get out the letters she had written as a child, all of which Marjorie had kept.

She could see herself growing up, the printed words of the child turning into a cursive script and then into an adult's handwriting.

On this her second visit to the Island, Joanna felt like a circle had been completed.

She smiled at her friend; "You know, the last time I was here I got engaged when I returned to New Zealand. It's different now that I don't have a man waiting for me when I return – I'm free to live my own life."

She dreamed of the willows, which meant she had to make a sad journey, but the willows also spoke of survival or rebirth.

The time went by all too quickly. A month later she was flying into the dawn on the return journey. She spoke to the Lord on the aircraft as her children slept.

"Father, I'm sad. I have left someone I love - and I'll probably not see her again, because she lives so far away."

Looking at her sleeping children tenderly she said, "Nothing else matters except these two. I feel like I'm going back to nothing. Help me to cope with the big 'nothing,' please."

The Lord's answer came from out of the dawn; "Nothing? I declare to you a new day ... and this is *not* the day of small things. You are going to go from 'cope' to 'hope'. There's a time for every purpose under heaven - and you are back for a purpose.

This is the land of your inheritance. If you can accept you belong there, you will find the reason I kept you in New Zealand."

As the plane touched down in Auckland, she had an instant of knowing that this was her time, and this was her place in the world.

On her return, she found a message the King had written her ten days before while she was still in the Isle of Wight,
I'm about to do a brand-new thing. See, I have already begun! – Isaiah 43:19

Something New,

I am going to bless you, so ignore the obstacles and keep walking. You're too important to me to be derailed by a situation that was only meant to give you character and direction.

It was grace that enabled you to make it this far, right? I have already proved that I can bring you through the fire without so much as the smell of smoke, and out of the lion's den without even a bite mark. If you're afraid of the future, check with the past. Have I failed you? No, and I never will!

My word to you today is, "I'm about to do a brand-new thing. See, I have already begun!" After feeling like you've waited forever, I will suddenly move, and if you're not ready you'll miss it.

I am getting ready to open some doors that have been closed to you; to break some chains that have held you back. I am saying, "I'm about to do a brand-new thing."

"Like what?" you ask. How about a new relationship, a new assignment, a new anointing, and a new approach to an old problem? I may not change, but I move. So get ready to move with me!

As soon as she recovered from jet-lag, the King told her to apply for a job at City College. She turned up the day they put the advertisement in the paper. They were surprised she'd turned up so early. "Is the advertisement already in the paper?" they asked.

"Uh, no" she replied, passing it off as coincidence. How could she explain the King guiding her in the way he did?

The interview was similar to the one she'd undergone five years before, even though it was with a different principal.

"I see you are a computer programmer, and you have Linux skills …" the principal said, looking at her resume. He wanted to hire her on the spot.

"Come with me, I'll take you to the technician you are replacing!" he announced.

 She was confused and taken aback. This was supposed to be a job interview – not a handover.

"Er, computer programming is a completely different skill-set from administering a computer network, looking after file servers and repairing computers," she said nervously.

He took no notice and continued with the handover. She followed him up the stairs wondering what she was getting herself into.

As they walked into the technician's room she stopped and stared.

Full circle

Joanna was standing in front of the man she'd replaced five years ago as a science technician. She knew him only as the brusque man who had not trained her. But she was aware that in the kingdom, he was a prince. She'd been attending his church ever since her return from Canberra.

They looked at each other, a silent understanding and fellowship passing between them. Speaking to the Lord silently, Joanna said; "Oh, *him* again. When did *he* return to City College? What are you *doing?*"

The prince was thinking along the same lines, wondering why their paths had crossed again. He was handsome, but she found him cold and stand-offish - and very northern looking compared to Ishmael.

His hair was now completely white, but the eyebrows over his earth-colored eyes were dark, and his unlined face was still young. His looks were those of a distinguished man not yet of middle age.

Feeling awkward, she stuffed her thoughts away for later and tried to appear calm, cool and collected.

They were showing her around the lab and she had not even agreed to take the job. If she took the job, she suspected they were about to be thrown together in a big way. Her emotions were a jumble of interest, excitement, hope and fear.

As she walked with the prince across the familiar school quadrangle, she experienced an intense feeling of déjà vu.

The beautiful big elm towered above them, now with new bright green leaves bursting from its branches.

"Oh, my God! What are you up to?" she questioned the King in her mind; "I'm back in the same place, following him again. Why am I following *him* around in a big circle?"

As the King's word from seven years ago at the levelled hill came to mind, she thought "This is the town I left. This is *full circle.*"

After the handover, the prince announced he was leaving that day. "Oh no, not again!" she said, staring at him in disbelief.

"Good Lord," she exclaimed, "Seriously, do you expect me to take this job without any training?"

The principal overheard her. Looking at her hopefully, he said, "You have Linux skills, and you learned to service computers in Canberra …"

"Yeah, why did I do that?" she whispered to the King, looking cornered.

"It's not my fault, I handed in my notice six weeks ago," the prince said to her quietly. It would have been around the time she left for the overseas trip. She couldn't believe that the job vacancy was not advertised until her return. It seemed the job had been waiting for her!

"Let me think about it over the weekend," she asked, knowing the King wanted her to take the job.

At home, she pulled her Bible out and studied the verses from Jeremiah 31:21-22 that she'd been given seven years ago. It was a promise that God would create a new thing in her life, after she'd gone around a man full circle.

Looking up every translation she could find, she analysed the last verse.

In one translation the word was 'encompass', which meant include in scope; include as part of something broader; have as one's sphere or territory; and in other translations the word 'compass' or 'encircle' meant to walk around a man in a circle.

Sitting down, she spoke to the King; "I know what I can see. This town is *'the town I left'* and *'walking around a man in a circle'* is what I did today! But I need your confirmation on this.

I am asking for your clearly revealed will, so there is no confusion or misunderstanding."

She put the Bible away. The King's silence was answer enough.

He never answered when it was obvious it was his will. Aligning herself with his will, she agreed to take the job and stay in the town.

She was hired on Monday, and on Wednesday she received the King's answer; an explanation of the final verse from Jeremiah 31:21-22 that had her baffled for seven years; *"The Lord will create a new thing on earth - a woman shall compass a man."*

The confirmation was of a very Jewish nature, which amused her. It took the form of a video at home group which showed what happens at a Jewish wedding.

The teacher, a Messianic Jew, explained that Jeremiah 31:21-22 meant the bride walking around the groom.

Prince Mentor

In November 2002 Joanna took the job at the College on the condition that she got some training from her predecessor. She told him about her decision – laying out her boundaries as she did so.

The atmosphere between them was prickly and tense.
"As far as I'm concerned, we have a business relationship, and we're both Christians. Being Christian sets up some pretty well-defined boundaries. I've been told by lots of women that they feel safe around me" the prince said earnestly, trying to put her at ease.

"I'm not 'lots of women,'" she retorted, but decided to give him the benefit of the doubt. He appeared to be an honest man. Eve knew him well and approved of him. She suspected the King definitely approved of him, judging from the way they'd been brought together.

Unfortunately, the prince was not interested in Joanna. He already had his sights set on a woman at church who he believed the King wanted him to marry.

"Things are moving along with the woman I'm interested in," he told her. Who was she? Joanna wondered. He always sat by himself at church. Where was she?

While laying out his boundaries he told Joanna that he did not want any 'uncomfortable moments', explaining he'd already had some 'uncomfortable moments' with a woman who'd believed he was God's chosen for her.

Annoyed with him, Joanna scowled. Who did he think he was? Why did he feel he needed to warn her off? There were probably going to be lots of 'uncomfortable moments.' She was already uncomfortable.

The King had placed them right in front of each other - and the first thing he'd done was put up a barrier. What would he do with the things the King seemed to be revealing to her? Why did he think she was there? He must have wondered.

Exasperated and put off, she built her own barriers, assuring him that he need not worry about her being 'interested.' It irked her that by stepping into this, she had to get to know him and rely on him as a mentor. They were now working together on a casual basis after she had insisted on some job training.

She had to make the professional relationship work, and was making the effort to get to know him on that level.

Joanna dubbed him 'Prince Mentor'. She did not trust him with her feelings.

The King heard of her worry;

"It is better to take refuge in the Lord than to trust in man, it is better to take refuge in the Lord than to trust in Princes." Psalm 118: 8-9 (NIV)

"Father, I don't even know if I like him. He is cold and distant, not putting out any signs, not putting himself at risk. I find him very presumptuous. He told me he knows who he's going to marry! He thinks you've told him everything that you've got mapped out for him in the next few years! If that were true, he'd know about me."

American eagle

Rolling her eyes and drumming her fingertips on the desk, Joanna hung onto the phone waiting for Prince Mentor to answer. She disliked having to depend on him and grimaced each time she rang. His tone was usually cold and unfriendly.

He complained she always managed to interrupt his shower or his shaving, no matter what time of the day she rang.

He did not try to undermine her, or make her look bad like her 'mentor' at the previous company. The only fault she found was that he could give long-winded explanations, and forget about traps for the unwary. There were plenty of them in their line of work.

"If not for you, I would have got away from here," she snapped while they were working together fixing some broken computers.

"Don't blame *me* for being kept here," he shot back.

"If you had not resigned, this job would not have come up, and we wouldn't be having this conversation!" she retorted, not daring to explain the King's will. She wanted to say "thrown together like this."

"It's too bad," he said shrugging; "Find out what you're here for! I have no sympathy."

"I know why I'm here – but you don't" she thought, holding her tongue.

"Have you lived in this town all your life?" Joanna asked at lunch.

"No, I'm American," he replied; "My father was a helicopter pilot in the US Army in Central America and South East Asia, and then he flew for a firm called Air America. At the end of the Vietnam War we settled in New Zealand."

An awkward silence followed. Prince Mentor looked at Joanna. She had a strange expression on her face.

"Where do you come from in the States?" Joanna casually asked, thinking "He's going to say *Florida*."

"I come from Florida," he replied.

Joanna nearly choked. "Oh, my God" she thought, as she stirred her cup of coffee, thinking of Isaac, the American husband the Lord had promised her – from Florida.

Prince Mentor watched the spoon go around and around in her cup. "I think your coffee is stirred," he said quizzically.

She listened distractedly as Prince Mentor talked about his childhood as an Air America Brat. Eve had said Prince Mentor had an interesting story about where he'd come from, but she hadn't taken much notice.
"So, the Chosen *is* American," she said to the King after work. "Who knew? His accent sounds like he was born and bred here, from the South Island perhaps. No, I am *not* going to tell him what you said. Stop smiling!"

Later, she dismissed it. She was simply reading too much into things. It was all just a lot of coincidences - one after the other. It was nothing, really. She had to keep both feet on the ground and watch that imagination. But the feeling wouldn't go away.

If Prince Mentor was Isaac, he wasn't looking in her direction.

"I find your actions hurtful, bringing me a prince who is indifferent to me. Isaac isn't interested in me, but Ishmael is ..." Joanna warned the King, looking back at the brown eyed, golden skinned man from Iraq, who still waited for her at the oasis.

She kept in daily contact with Ishmael. He was a salve to her wounded ego.
It appeared that both men had been summoned from a far-off land. Perhaps the King meant Isaac when he said *"From the east I summon a bird of prey."* Both kingdoms of Ishmael and Isaac bore an eagle for their symbol. Ishmael's was a golden black eagle and Isaac's was an American bald eagle.

Iraq and America were on the news every day - they were fighting each other in the second Gulf War. When the war started the King warned there would be a clash of civilisations. On a personal level he said Iraq represented Ishmael while America represented Isaac.

Which man would fulfill the King's purpose for her? Her wounded heart already knew the answer.
Above her, the eagle flew.

A message from the King

Prince Mentor's indifference caused Joanna to take refuge in the desert.

"Why have you led me on this path?" she asked the King, as she shouldered the load of her household and the work Prince Mentor left her.

"You chose it," he replied; "I gave you the choice, and you chose the hard yet interesting path."

She thought about it as she followed the King up a dry mountain pass. The path was certainly getting interesting.

"When Prince Mentor wakes up to what your plans are - will he approve of me?" she asked the Lord, wondering if she still needed a man's approval; "At least I have *your* approval. I thirst for that from you."

Tired and thirsty, she stopped for a rest.

"I spread out my hands to you; my soul thirsts for you like a parched land," she said, speaking the words from Psalm 143:6.

"It is dry up here. Where's this living water you spoke of?" she asked.

"You will find it," the King answered.

At the close of the year the King sent to both her and Prince Mentor a message;

You... Became My Partners

"You can't do it by yourself" the message read;

A woman was in a situation where she needed help but kept shouting, 'I'll do it myself!'" Are you like that? Trying to do it all on your own?

On his office wall, Alex Haley, the author of Roots, has a picture of a turtle sitting on top of a six-foot fence post. The caption reads, "You can be sure he had help getting up there!" Haley says, "Anytime I feel too proud to ask for help, I look at that picture."

Somebody within your reach knows something you need to know; something you'll never learn on your own. They're your mentor. Get close to them. Drop your bucket into their well and begin to draw water.

Paul recognised his limitations so he connected his life to others.

Listen, "You Philippians became my partners in giving and receiving. "Some of us know how to give but not receive. Others know how to receive but not give. Winners know how to do both!" Philippians 4:15

After reading the message she walked onto the back porch and spoke to the King;
"Yes, it's funny about the post turtle, but Father - why do you think I am too proud to ask for help? At my last job I wasn't too proud, I was too scared!
You saw what happened when I did ask. I was accused of asking the same question twice, of not asking the right question, of not 'thinking outside the box' - whatever that cliché meant, they wouldn't explain.
You know of the times when I asked and I was ignored, given the wrong information, not given enough information, refused, sabotaged, or made to look like a fool."
"I witnessed it," the King replied; "It hurt to see it ... and your response. I watched you withdraw and try your best to do the task by yourself, leaving yourself in a very precarious situation."
She asked, "What do you want me to do?"

"Be assertive," he replied; "Do not be afraid to ask for help at your new job, even if you have to insist on it."
He outlined the practical part to her first; "You are to get Prince Mentor to assist you next month at work. It is too large a job getting the computer lab and library ready for the new school term on your own.
When you go to the principal with your request, get Deborah to pray while you are in his office. Prince Mentor will provide you with a strategy to use when you ask for help."
"As you wish," she replied, bowing to him

Walking into the Kingdom, she found the path that led to the well that the King had spoken of. "What do you mean about the mentor, the bucket and the well?" she asked.
"Is it not obvious?" the King replied smiling; "You both know something the other needs to know; something you'll never learn on your own. You need to learn from each other. I have confirmed he is your mentor. He is honest - and he has a deep well of knowledge and understanding which he is happy to share. It's alright to get close to him."
Joanna looked askance at the King; "Is he the one? If he is, he does not see me," she warned.
"He will," the King replied.

Following the path, she found herself at the top of the steep hill she had struggled up the previous day. The oasis of Ishmael was far away now, a little glint of silver in the distance.

Leading her to the well the King handed her a bucket.

The Well of Salvation

Joanna could see the King as the water-pourer from the pages of the Bible; "*Let anyone who is thirsty come to me and drink*" he said, making his appeal in a loud voice.

The Festival of Tabernacles was a feast he'd designed for his chosen people to remind them of their forty years of desert wandering after the Exodus.

On the last and greatest day of the seventh and final feast, the Jews drew water and poured it out before the Lord. Joanna read in John 7:37 that he watched them saying; *"Whoever believes in me, as Scripture has said, rivers of living water will flow from within them."*

In the dry and weary land of the earth, only he could give living water and satisfy a thirsty spirit.

Guided by the King, Joanna had come to the second of a series of desert wells.

"With joy you will draw water from the wells of Salvation," he'd promised … but she did not have any joy at drawing the water from this well, only frustration and confusion.

The day after she'd found the well, Prince Mentor invited Joanna to a New Year's Eve party, making it clear he wasn't asking her out. She decided to go, taking Eve. At the party, Prince Mentor told her the woman he *had* wanted to come had not turned up.

Put off, and dubbing him "Prince Charmless" Joanna decided to see the New Year of 2003 in at Eve's place.

She walked out without saying goodnight, leaving Eve to tell him she was leaving.

Later, she went back to the King fuming.

"I don't like him," she snapped, throwing the bucket away; "He knows nothing! I am not thirsty for the water from that well. It is bitter."

The King sighed in exasperation as he handed the bucket back.

Joanna felt rejected.

"Right now, I don't like Prince Charmless, or even you for that matter. He is telling me you have chosen *someone else* for him. Where does that leave me?" she asked.

"I am sorry, that was not my will," the King consoled her.

"Is this Isaac, the one that you promised comes after Ishmael?" she asked; "I know that Isaac means laughter – but he is not making me laugh. Every time I see him, he talks about the mystery woman he's interested in – but there's no sight of her and I would have expected to see her on New Year's Eve.

Why does he think I'm interested in his love life? I told him right at the start not to discuss romance or church at work! He hasn't listened. Is he telling me all this stuff so I'll keep my distance?"

"He thinks you're genuinely interested in what he has to say. Either ignore him, or tell him that you don't want to hear it," the King counselled.

"If I do that, I fear he may not be helpful to me at work" she replied.

Instead, annoyed at him, she sent him a message that was designed to get back at him; "I am so glad you've got a girlfriend. It makes it easier for me to relax around men when I know they've got someone and aren't interested in me. I look forward to meeting her. Oh, by the way, where was she at New Year?"

"There, go analyze that" she snapped with a disdainful look on her face; "See how interested I am in you – NOT."

Justifying herself to the King who was shaking his head and sighing she said; "Well, if he is telling the truth, he need not worry about ME, for I still love Ishmael and I'm waiting for Isaac, the man you promised. HE can't be Isaac.

If he is playing a game, and lying through his back teeth, then as far as I am concerned, he deserves what I'm dishing out. I can play that game too."

The King looked at her with disapproval.

"Father, what do you want me to do?" she asked, exasperated.

"Let righteousness guard your heart, not deception" the King chided.

"Well, why don't you tell this *wonderful* prince you've found me that as well? He is supposed to hear you," she replied angrily.

The Deceptive Brook

"How do you know the woman you call your lady friend is the one for you? She doesn't even sit with you at church," Joanna challenged Prince Mentor.

"All the signs and prophetic words I've been given point to her. She will sit with me when she is ready" he replied.

Irked, Joanna did not reply.

When she was on her own, she went to find the King. Fuming, she kicked the bucket down the hill. She saw it hid a ledge. She went down and gave it another good kick, making sure it went all the way to the bottom.

Swinging around, she met the King, her eyes lit green with anger and defiance; "*You said* he was the one, but *he said* you have someone else for him."

The King made his reply from Proverbs 16:1; *"To man belong the purposes of the heart, from the King comes the reply of the tongue."*

"Well, I don't want to be here at this well!" Joanna objected. "How can I ever learn to trust either of you?

If I go on the plain meaning of his words my map is wrong, or you're a liar. If I go on the signs you've given me, then *he* is the liar. I'm getting out of this."

"You have to wait. We're not moving on," the King replied.

"Have you gone mad?" she asked. "He appears to have all the signs of Isaac, but he's not. Thanks for the mind game that I do not need right now. You are killing me. Thanks for bringing him to me – NOT!"

"Come here" the Lord said, wanting to bring her some solace. He could see how the dragon had been mocking her.

Sighing, she swung around again, her eyes still green.

The King and Prince Mentor were driving her crazy.

"Why is my pain unending and my wound grievous and incurable? Will you be to me like a deceptive brook? Like a spring that fails?" she asked, using the words from Jeremiah 15:18.

"My word is true, and I am watching to see it accomplished. I cannot lie" he said.

She looked down. The bucket was back at her feet.

In the heavens the hot January sun was entering the sign of Aquarius, the water bearer.

"I'm sorry," she said shading her eyes; "I don't like this place. Please lead me away from here."

"Come with me," the King replied.

"Where are we going?" she asked.

"Back to the well," he replied.

Sighing, she climbed the hill.

Walking back to the well, she looked in. It was deep. Drinking the life-giving water, she stepped back as Prince Mentor approached. He had been sending her messages.

Circling each other warily, they began to talk.

"Did you see the message from the Lord at New Years?" he asked.

It seemed the King had spoken to him as well. When he read it, he'd been amused at the King's words, wondering what her reaction would be.

"You do not know the half of it," she thought, watching him with her lips sealed.

She needed his knowledge at work, but he needed her knowledge of the Kingdom.

He was her mentor, but she was the one within his reach who knew something he needed to know; something he'd never learn on his own.

Sparks and sparring

Sparks flew between Princess Joanna and Prince Mentor, but they were not sparks of attraction.
As iron sharpens iron, so one person sharpens another. Proverbs 27:17

Prince Mentor didn't know the things the King had revealed to Joanna about him. She was a closed book who kept her dreams and visions to herself.

The King was not impressed with all the sparring.
"What did I do?" Joanna spread out her hands helplessly; "I'm not being dishonest. I'm not saying anything. Don't tell me off, it's his fault."

The King replied "You are hiding. You cannot wear deception over righteousness. If you want him for a friend, then *be* a friend."
"An honest answer is a sign of true friendship ... it is like a kiss on the lips," he added, quoting from Proverbs 24:26.

"Oh really," Joanna scowled; "How can I tell him who I am? I did not start this – HE did. He said he did not want any uncomfortable moments! You heard him. He has gotten off on the wrong foot with me right from the start. As for sparring - why don't you go and tell him to stop sparring and be a friend to *me*?" The King chose to ignore her rebellious attitude.

Joanna wondered how to be pleasant without revealing anything. Prince Mentor might not know where he was going, but the gift of discernment was very strong in him. She sensed he was trying to draw her out. The better they got to know each other, the more uncomfortable it grew.

Joanna hid the things the King had disclosed concerning him, but it was becoming increasingly difficult. She did not feel safe revealing anything about the Kingdom, especially where he appeared in it. The King had shown him the well, but he did not know the significance of the circle where their paths kept crossing, or that the Lord had promised her an American husband.

Chapter Eight

Prince Mentor walked into Joanna's lab later in the day. Ishmael was on her mind and she let something slip about him.

He slowly said, "That is significant. I have been told about Ishmael."

"I never meant to say anything about Ishmael. I don't even know how that came out," Joanna replied.

"I understand how it came out. I was meant to hear that. It will be a test of your trust in me," he replied smiling.

She hated it when men demanded her trust, but let it pass. Wary, she waited to see how he would treat her before she decided about trust.

The things the King had shown her were kept to herself. She was not ready to reveal all she knew.

"What does Ishmael mean to you?" she asked.

"Ishmael was conceived before God had made the covenant of circumcision with Abram. This covenant marked the point at which Abram became Abraham. The addition of the H denotes the breath of God, and by implication the holiness of God. Abraham asked God to bless Ishmael, which God did. God's covenant was with Isaac though.

Then God's promise to Abraham about having a son named Isaac came to pass. The Hebrew meaning for Ishmael is, 'God will hear.' Isaac means laughter," he replied.

She relaxed, hearing from his reply that he didn't know what Ishmael meant to her specifically. Choosing a safer subject, she talked about the others on her path;

"The only difference is that with the others, I have picked and chosen who joins me. Lately I've not been given a lot of choice!"

"You mean he has chosen for you!" he replied.

Why did he say the King had chosen for her? She shot a quick look at the King. Had he revealed anything to him about being chosen?

"He's bringing you to a point where you will have to face some issues. When you chose who walked with you it was possible to avoid those issues," Prince Mentor continued.

She couldn't ask what the chosen meant to him.

"What are you talking about?" she asked instead; "My gut feeling is you are normally open and honest, but you're holding something back. I can and I will figure it out."

"As for holding something back … yes and no," he replied; "As you start to understand the prophetic gift you will realise why this is so. He has shown me stuff that I can't tell you, hut he will in his time. I can tell you that his revelations help me from taking offense. Essentially it gives me grace to handle the 'tantrums.'"

He revealed, "I'm sharing part of a prophetic word over me, which should also give you more insight into what is happening … 'God says "For you have the ability to touch those that others can't reach. You have the ability to really reach out to some that others don't even want to be a part of. ....

For God says 'I'm releasing even within you the healing anointing that you can be able to walk with the heart that needs to be mended, needs to be made right, needs to be made whole.' For He's taken away the hurts, and the pains, and the sorrows, and the frustrations....' So as you can see, I'm only following part of His calling for me."

The King bid her step forward to reveal the Kingdom and the princess within. Gingerly coming out of hiding, she revealed who she was.

Showing him her map, she explained, "At the start of my journey the Lord told me to set up signs and mark the road, and I did. I used the bible to do it. I use it as a map - that's how I know where I am, and what this is.

I use a Kingdom story, which is my safe place where I can go to work out stuff with him, interpret the signs, get rid of dragons, and correct my walk."

"His word is the atlas. He gives me dreams and visions as mud maps," Prince Mentor replied.

He smiled as he added, "So that's how I know where I am. He also gave me a good dose of discernment."

Stunned, she said "I feel like I'm going into a different world a part of me knows, but never dreamed would come true. The Kingdom was a place where I could go, hear from my Father the King, and work out stuff in the outside world - it was a story!!! I am shocked to see it become real. Oh, what have I done?"

"You haven't done anything," Prince Mentor replied; "Remember this saying; *'Courage is fear that has said its prayers.'*"

As Joanna described Isaac, she kept the circle and Isaac's role hidden.

"In the story, Isaac's the one who knows the King, bows to him, is taught by him, understands scripture, wears armour, and has conquered the dragon in bloody battles, yet laughs easily.

Isaac knows the desert, for he has lived there too. He's Ishmael's younger brother, but the inheritance is his. He is my equal," she explained, before telling him about Ishmael.

"Ishmael I met while walking through the desert. He believes our book the Bible has been changed and as a consequence he will not accept my witness, or the truth about the King. I know the Father's word never returns empty, and I ask the Father that he will come to know the King like we do. I pray that he will know the truth, and the truth will set him free."

She showed him the places where she existed and walked with the King; "The desert is a harsh place; it leads to places like Samaria and Ishmael. I'd been choosing the wrong places to go to satisfy my thirst. The only well I knew was at Samaria, and I didn't want to go back there, nor could I go to Ishmael. Taking me back to Samaria, the Lord showed me the woman at the well and taught me about living water. He showed me what to thirst for.

I said, 'the well is deep, and there is no cup.' So anyway, I seem to have ended up here, with a bucket - when a cup would have done; a mentor I have to get close to, and a well that I did not trust … because I thought it was deceptive. I didn't trust you, so I had to test the waters. I am wary and here be dragons. I don't know who I am yet in the Kingdom story I write."

Prince Mentor introduced Isaac as he replied; "That confirmed most of what I had been shown. I did miss a couple of details, though I wasn't surprised because they fit the scenario. Remember, Isaac has fought those dragons too."

Noting that he named himself as 'Isaac', Joanna cautiously tested the waters.

"I know who you are," she said, watching him.

Mistaking his mentoring role, he replied; "Prince Mentor. There's an irony to this that makes me laugh each time I see him work like this."

Then he indicated where he wanted to go with her, "Some of Isaac's mentors may appear to be dragons at first. You may be required to give them trust as well. Only time will tell on that score.

To be scared is fine; just don't let a spirit of fear take control. He never intended our walk to be a stroll in the park. We will have mountains and valleys to traverse; we just have to ask him to be there with us."

What did he mean by 'Isaac's mentors?' She grew uneasy. Where was this going?

Then he went completely off track; "You realise, that when things develop further with my lady friend, I will have to let her know about the 'mentoring.' NOT THE DETAILS, just the fact that it is happening, and perhaps who is being mentored.
You don't need to worry about this, but you do need to know where I stand. I will be making myself accountable to pastoral / eldership oversight on this. No details, but my accountability person will know who it is. I'm praying who that oversight should be.
If this is unacceptable, let me know, and mentoring will cease forthwith."

Joanna realized that although he heard nearly everything, he understood nothing ... and was still focused on his imaginary lady friend!

She had shared nearly every precious thing the King had given her - and watched him trample it underfoot!

Who did he think he was? After the grief came anger. How *dare* he try to take control? What did he intend to construct, another triangle?

"What are you talking about?" she asked, growing angrier by the minute, as she threw the bucket down the hill.

"I only need you to mentor me at work!" she snapped, putting him in his place. "I don't want any other mentoring from you, I already have a mentor and she is a woman. You shouldn't even be thinking of mentoring women, especially when you are single. It is not appropriate! I can look after myself and I don't need you to rescue me!" she added.

After putting him in his place, she retreated into fuming silence and sulked.

He could see the door was closed.

"I believe you are missing it as far as the mentoring thing is concerned," he said, misunderstanding his role; "I recognise it is my role to show you where healing can be found. Perhaps give you some insight as well. We obviously have different definitions of mentoring."

"Obviously," she fumed. This prince thought she needed rescuing, not courting.

Angry, she went looking for the King. "Why did you tell me to reveal the Princess to him?" she asked. "I nearly told him he was Isaac!"

"My daughter, courage is not the absence of fear, but rather the judgment that something else is more important than fear," the King replied while her daughter was watching the Princess Diaries; "From now one you will be travelling the road between who you think you are and who you can be. The key is to allow yourself to make the journey."

Choosing the Chosen

"Oh, no!" Joanna said, aghast, as she went running for the King; "As soon as I shut the door on Isaac, Ishmael's appeared. He says he wants to be with me and he'll be flying over from Australia!"

It didn't occur to her that she should have stopped talking to Ishmael.

"You know what you must do," the King replied; "It is time to make that choice we spoke of. Choose 'the chosen.' You must choose now."

"Do you know what you're asking me to do?" Joanna cried; "The one you've chosen doesn't want me!"

The King was silent.

"Isaac does not want me, Ishmael does!" she repeated.

"This is so hard" she said to herself, shaking her head; "Why must I choose a man who rejects me?"

If she knew about the chosen, then it followed that the chosen would know about *her*. That was her presumption.

She had not foreseen that Isaac would have a love interest. She had known that Prince Mentor, with his 'lady friend' was Isaac right from the start, from the signs the King had given - signs that had been very clear and specific. Prince Mentor himself had confirmed he was Isaac.

Bowing to the King, she chose Isaac. In her mind this was choosing rejection. She wanted a man who wanted her. So far, all Isaac had done was trample all over her self-esteem. Ishmael wanted her, but she knew how wrong that was.

"Don't trust your emotions" she counseled herself, as she sang a song the King had made her learn by heart from Proverbs 3:5 (NKJ),

Trust in the Lord with all your heart, and lean not on your own understanding;
in all your ways acknowledge Him, and He shall direct your paths.

She sought the King, "Look, I am going your way, even though I disagree with your choice.

I find Ishmael to be far more attractive. He was head and shoulders above the rest and had no equal in my affections. He was the one who restored my self-esteem and got me back on my feet. Until Isaac came, he had my heart."

The King replied "You are right not to trust your preference for Ishmael."

"The heart is deceitful above all things and beyond cure. Who can understand it?" he added, quoting from Jeremiah 17:9.

Joanna agreed, "Yes, and for that reason I will trust you rather than my injured feelings. You know my heart. I want what you want. I've chosen Isaac."

The King smiled. "Now we wait …."

She did not have long to wait. Ishmael received her reply and let her go … and even though he was jealous, he wished her all the best with 'Isaac.' Even though she wanted to run into his arms and tell him in her misery it was *all wrong*, she had chosen someone who did not exist for her, she held back and kept silent. They would always be friends and she knew she had his respect.

Letting go of Ishmael, she prayed Abraham's words, *"If only Ishmael might live under your blessing!"* Genesis 17:18

"Yes, I will surely bless him" the Lord agreed, "but my covenant is with Isaac."

Staring into the night sky, she looked at the constellation of the Southern Cross. Its name was Crux, meaning "the cross endured." Disappearing from Jerusalem's sky after the King's death and resurrection, the constellation was not seen again until the sixteenth century, when voyagers rounded the Cape of Good Hope bringing back news of "a wonderful cross more glorious than all the constellations of the heavens."

"Day after day the constellations pour forth speech, night after night they reveal knowledge," she said, lifting her head and quoting the Word from Psalm 19.

Ishmael had come to the great southern lands of Crux, the Southern cross. Did he ever ask himself why there was such freedom in New Zealand and Australia? Her nation had been built on Christianity. Her national anthem was one big long prayer to the God of nations.

The cross was in the sign of Libra, the scales. In Ismael's language it was Al Zubena, meaning purchase or redemption. Three bright stars explained its meaning.

The first star, Alpha, named Zuben al Genubi, meant *the purchase, or the price is deficient.* Beta, the second star, named Zuben al Chemali, meant *the price which covers.* Gamma, the third star, named Zuben Akrabi meant *the price of the conflict.*

She knew the King had paid the price;
*"Christ bought us with His blood and made us free from the Law. In that way, the Law could not punish us. Christ did this by carrying the load and by being punished instead of us. It is written, "Anyone who hangs on a cross is hated and punished." Because of the price Christ Jesus paid, the good things that came to Abraham might come to the people who are not Jews.
And by putting our trust in Christ, we receive the Holy Spirit He has promised. Galatians 3:13-15, GNT.*

"May Ishmael come to know the power and wisdom of the cross" she asked, fearing it would be a stumbling block for him.

"Jews demand signs and Greeks look for wisdom, but we preach Christ crucified: a stumbling block to Jews and foolishness to Gentiles, but to those whom God has called, both Jews and Greeks, Christ the power of God and the wisdom of God. For the foolishness of God is wiser than human wisdom, and the weakness of God is stronger than human strength." 1 Corinthians 1:22-25.

The next day she thought of the choice she'd made between Ishmael and Isaac. One knew the King, one did not. One was chosen; one was not. One she knew, the other would have to be on blind faith.

Nothing was said to Isaac. Joanna had gone back to hiding behind her work and professional mask. On the very same day she let go of Ishmael, Prince Mentor was also rejected by his lady friend.

Joanna heard about it at work the next morning. Although chastened he did not seem all that upset. Covering her wonder at the timing she laughed, making a jibe about Prince Mentor's map, saying it must have been wrong if his lady friend had not seen 'the big sign in the sky.'

Isaac looked at her, dumbfounded at her lack of sympathy.

Stung, he replied "Well, there's plenty of choice after her. I already have someone else, but I don't think you'll want to hear *that*."

He was right! His words found their mark.

"Why did you even say that? Are you fishing for some response from me?" she asked tersely, glaring at him.

"Fishing? No …" he replied, his open and honest face flushed with consternation.

Downing her tools, she stomped off to the staff room with her coffee cup.

"Why are you angry?" Prince Mentor asked, following her down the corridor.

'Not telling you …' she thought, finding another reason to get mad at him.

Rounding on him in the staff room, Joanna said, "Listen, I don't care about your love life! I told you right at the start of our working relationship to leave that man-woman stuff out of work and we'd get along fine. You haven't done that!"

Who did he think he was - God's gift to women? Prince Charming, he was not. She wished that once the day's work was over, the King would send him far, far away. Iceland would be good.

The King left them to it. It took all of her patience to deal with him in her usual smooth manner. The work did not progress, the day went badly, and she was not there for her children after school.

The King told her of her worth, to believe in herself and not to let it get to her.

"You are the gold," he said. If that was true, then why could Prince Mentor not see it?

"Please, I think this Isaac thing has gone far enough," she said to the King, giving him the story. "You heard him. His signs, prophetic words and dreams all pointed to his 'lady friend.' If it be your will, then please release him from the story.

Let him have what his words have made real. Get me out of this - and find me what I do need. I don't know what you're doing!

Is being treated like this what I need? Father, you're hurting me. What did I do that was so wrong that I should be treated like this? Why did you give me a stone when I asked for bread? I didn't ask you for a bad thing."

She felt bewildered and lost. Isaac plus lady friend had caused her map to make no sense … and if the signs were wrong, now she didn't know where she was. It was like she was standing on magnetic rock that rendered her compass useless.

In front of her, all she could see was the vast, trackless desert. With no landmarks or reliable map, there was no way home.

Picking up her shield of faith, which now bore the symbol of the covenant promise, she spoke to the King; "Perhaps I was relying more on the signs than I was on *you*. If the signs, dreams and prophetic words that he received do not point to me, then my signs must have been wrong.

How, I do not know, for they couldn't have been clearer. Anyway, if my signs were wrong, then please reveal it to me and lead me on a safe path.

I'm sorry I was more interested in the signs being right than I was in this *wonderful* prince you found me - please forgive me my sarcasm. I 'm sorry I got impatient with him. I know his rejection of me is not your rejection of me.

Anyway, it doesn't matter, as long as you love me. I do want this prophetic gift but it is a hard thing to swallow when I see things and know things that I did not wish or choose for myself. Help me to take care when handling your Word.

You know, the desert is not so bad - look at what I've learned in the dry land.

Please help me to forget Ishmael, for I know I can't look back. And please help me to forget Isaac, the one I had hoped for, because I can't look forward.

Iliafi said 'let the days speak to us.' These days speak to me of Ishmael and Isaac, of rejection and dragons and impossible choices. Help me to slay the dragons and live in the present. I can make it on my own, as long as you are with me.

Your Shepherds rod and staff, it comforts me."

After swallowing her disappointment and settling for the desert, Joanna bowed and walked away.

Issac

"Tell Isaac of the choice you made," the King said, fixing his eyes upon Joanna as he made his outrageous demand.

"Oh, no, no, no" she said, shaking her head vehemently and pulling back, "No! I'd rather die. Please don't ask me to do that. Come and kill me now."

He did not let her run far. "You must. Give him that chapter. If he is on the same page, he should know!" he said, getting in front of her.

"NO! I can't" she shouted.

The King insisted, so she clapped her hands over her ears and ran from him, going; "La-la-La-la, La-la-La-la, I can't hear you!"

"Yes, you can … and I am waiting!" he called after her.

The King's voice nagged at her all weekend. At church, the teaching was about 'presumption.'

Joanna avoided Isaac. At the end of the service, she chose the side door as an exit.

Isaac sent her a message, "Are you still talking to me?"

She didn't reply.

The King got in front of her, stern and unyielding, his eyes flashing, "Who gives you breath? Who governs the Kingdom? Who gave you that promise?

Who gives you this gift of story-telling and interpretation of signs? Who brought Isaac onto your path? It was I, and I require your obedience and your trust. Now do it!"

The argument raged on, "You are killing me. I'd rather have my teeth pulled!" Joanna groaned out loud, as she went to collect her daughter Nicole.

When she arrived at the place where her daughter was staying, her friend's mother told her she was applying for a job at *a dentist's surgery*. Then the mother said her daughter was *having her tooth pulled*.

The King stood there waiting. He knew how obstinate Joanna could be.

Forced to pay attention to the warning sign, she surrendered. Joanna wrote the chapter in such a way that if Prince Mentor chose, he could just treat it as a story. She sent the chapter off that night, her finger hesitating and trembling over the 'send' key.

"I'm afraid that he'll trample the pearls underfoot the way the Minstrel did," she groaned, worried.

"He won't," the King replied, telling her a story;

"The kingdom of heaven is like a merchant seeking beautiful pearls, who when he had found one pearl of great price, went and sold all that he had and bought it." Matthew 13:45

"He is not a pig" the King reassured the anxious princess. He has been waiting for you for a long time … and like the merchant in my tale; he will know the value of what he has found."

The next morning, Prince Mentor got straight back to Joanna saying; "Read this first - about presumption. God is infallible. What God shows me, and what I believe don't always match.

Therefore, I have to go back to what he shows me, for clarification of his will and direction. I'm human and prone to making mistakes, especially when it is something "I" want." Take what you want out of this and leave the rest."

He added; "The message about presumption really spoke to me. I suspect it spoke to you as well."

Joanna could see he was bemused by the story. Very interested in what she had given him, Isaac asked; "Prince Mentor and Isaac, are they the same person? Prince Mentor and Isaac, do they fill the same role? Is the Chosen the same as Prince Mentor and Isaac?"

"Yes, no and yes", Joanna replied, wondering where this was going.

"It is an impressive answer to prayer," Prince Mentor replied, as he came back with another question about the role Isaac would play; "So am I to understand that Prince Mentor / Isaac and the Princess will be united some way in the Kingdom?"

Joanna chose not to reply.

He continued, "A long time before you came along, I asked and prayed for the King's will to be done.

I don't necessarily understand what is happening, but I do know his will is being done. If you think he has shown you certain things keep them to yourself, and let him do the work."

Smiling, Joanna replied "You don't have to tell me to keep things to myself."

Happy with her, the King quoted from the Song of Solomon 8:5, asking *"Who is this coming up from the wilderness leaning on her beloved?"*

The desert behind her, Joanna replied from Romans 8:28-30;

"For to those who love God, who are called in his name, everything works out, for good. And God himself chose them, to bear the likeness of his son, that they may be the first of many, many brothers and sisters. What, then, shall I say in response to this ... If God be for us, who can be against us?"

The courtship

Although Joanna had not 'fallen in love' with Isaac, he had her liking and respect. From the start she preferred Isaac over Ishmael, because of his allegiance to the King. Her heart held no secrets, only shadows. She felt peace and a deep contentment that went beyond all understanding. All was well with her soul.

Their courtship began slowly. They spent the first six weeks building boundaries and coming to an agreement with each other about their conduct, visiting and the children. It was different from the dating she'd attempted out in the world. They did not sleep together, instead they chose to honour the King and wait.

Of necessity the courtship included the children, who the King regarded as fatherless. The children, who had always known that Isaac would one day come, were gracious to him and welcomed him.

The way they saw it, his had been the empty chair at the dinner table. In turn Isaac cared for the children and started to forge deep bonds with them.

Joanna visited Isaac with her children. He lived in an old cottage just off the beach, in a street sheltered by Norfolk pines and black sand dunes. The rolling waves of the Tasman could be heard, sometimes a soft murmur, other times a loud roar.

One day she walked into his old cottage at his invitation, following him into the kitchen as he made coffee. He leaned against the bench holding out his arms for her.

As she folded herself into his arms, she smiled. Her head fitted just beneath his chin.

"Thanks for keeping yourself in shape" Isaac said as he smiled down at her.

"Same to you" she replied, smiling.

He wasn't big on compliments. She preferred his honesty to the charm of Silver-tongue and Ishmael.

Isaac ticked all the boxes – the only thing he lacked was money.

He'd made a start on renovating his tidy cottage but had been unable to continue, clearly. His old car was in the same tired condition as his house.

Joanna stayed silent at church about their relationship. At the end of summer, just after the courtship began, a woman came to visit her home group. The stranger, a Scots woman who lived in Florida, came bearing a gift for them all – a word of knowledge for every person there.

When it came time for Joanna to receive her word, the woman bid her and the man sitting next to her to come forward. Shaking her head, Joanna declared; "No, I'm not with him, I'm on my own."

"You are not on your own ..." the prophet spoke to Joanna in her rich Scottish brogue; "There is a man, and you are going to be married. You've asked the Lord about that man, is he the one? Yes, he *is* the one God has chosen. He has been waffling, but now he knows!

You have come from a very hard place. Your life has been like a desert. The desert is going to bloom. You are precious, very precious to Him.

You used to have very bad nightmares. You will never be bothered by those again. You have dreams. God will speak to others out of these dreams."

The room went silent as every eye was fastened on Joanna. The prophet moved to the next person, saying "… the almond trees are in bloom, they are in bloom."

Joanna tried hard to keep her feelings in check, but gave up as her chin quivered and tears started to flow. The joy and wonder could not be contained. She knew the King had paid her a very deep honour, and she thanked the prophet for delivering the word he had given her. There was no way the Scots woman could have known anything about Joanna or her life.

When she came back to earth, she grinned. Joanna had not been ready to reveal anything to anybody at home group about Isaac.

Now their courtship had been announced despite her best efforts at keeping it quiet - and the whole church would soon know.

As soon as she got home the joy bubbled over. She laughed as she delivered the King's message to Isaac.

Isaac proposes

"My mother's maiden name is 'Isaacson'" Isaac told Joanna.

"Now why doesn't that surprise me? You are Isaac from Florida, dressed up as Bret from Wanganui!" Joanna exclaimed laughing.

"I suppose the next thing will be for us to get engaged," Isaac said looking at Joanna, his face reflecting his happiness. Joanna thought it was a bit sudden.

"You don't have enough money for a ring," she replied dubiously, thinking it would take him years to save for it.

Isaac had no income. Years ago, when the King had stopped her on the mountain asking her to list the qualities and attributes of the chosen - she forgot to mention money. The King obviously did not think money was important.

"Don't tempt God" Isaac replied, smiling.

The King agreed with Isaac, handing him a very beautiful, expensive ring which had come from Isaac's grandmother in Clearwater, Florida.

She was still alive, although now a widow and she loved the King. Her second husband had given her the ring when he proposed, and her marriage had been happy.

Isaac held onto the ring until the time was right. One winter afternoon he bounded in, wanting Joanna to watch the sunset. It was indeed a beautiful sunset. The King provided the setting, painting the sky red and gold.

Mt Taranaki stood to the west, a small triangle jutting out against the fiery horizon. He urged Isaac to get Joanna there quickly. Hand in hand, they walked to the tower at the end of the street that overlooked the town and river.

Isaac looked down at her, his expression tender as he proposed. When she said yes, he slid the ring on her finger and kissed her. It fit perfectly, as if made for her. The ring held a single diamond, over a carat, on a slim gold band. It did not need a fancy setting - the beauty was in the diamond.

"Is the diamond big enough?" the King asked smiling, reminding her of the day at the deer park when she'd said "it had better be a big diamond!"

"It's perfect," she replied happily.

Shelter in the storm

Anxious, Joanna looked out the window, grimacing at the wind gusts that rocked the house as huge storms lashed the lower half of the North Island. She was going to get married the next day.

She sat at the kitchen table with her sister Luka on the eve of her wedding, while the wild wind blew outside, and storm clouds chased each other across the sky.

"Do you think the storm will stop by tomorrow?" Luka, the Matron of Honour asked.

"I don't know," Joanna groaned, throwing the King a worried look as she addressed him directly. "God, I need you to do something about this storm! Can you make it stop, like you did when you were in the boat with your disciples? I want the sunshine and the cicadas. You're the only one who can settle the weather!"

The day of the wedding, the 21st of February 2004, arrived grey and stormy. They prayed for the storm to stop, as did every person in the Kingdom attending the wedding.

Guests from out of town navigated floods, closed roads and fallen trees.

Finally, it was time to travel to the garden. The wind abated, and by the time the car pulled in, the weather became calm. Joanna gathered her children to her just before they entered the garden, telling them how grateful she was for them, and thanking them for all the good they'd brought her in the years she'd been alone.

The solitary path ended at the garden and a new path began. She walked over the green lawn on her son's arm to Isaac, the man with the white hair who waited for her.

The storm battered the land outside the trees, but inside the garden the air was still and expectant.

The sun came out in all its brilliance as the King made his entrance. They'd invited him to the wedding and he made his presence felt. Sunlight filled the garden. Isaac kept his eyes on her and she saw the emotion and light on his face.

As they made their vows, two monarch butterflies fluttered in the still air in front of them.

Incredulous at the calm in the storm, the guests asked, "Did you see the butterflies, as you were making your vows?"

After the wedding ceremony, they made their way into town, where their reception was held indoors at the town civic centre.

The storm rolled in again, after the wedding reception ended and they left for their honeymoon. Their journey was interrupted by falling trees, which the wind snapped in half and threw on the road.

Joanna studied Isaac's handsome profile while they were stopped waiting for the road to be cleared. "I hope our marriage is not going to be this stormy!" she remarked.

Smiling, Isaac replied "Well our courtship certainly was! I am sure the storms will end now that we are married."

The weather was calm at the lodge they stayed at by the banks of the Tongariro River, but when they left another storm struck and the river swept through the grounds. It seemed the King protected them from the worst of it.

"He calmed the storm to a whisper and stilled the waves." (Psalm 107:29)

Turning north

The elevator doors opened and Joanna stepped out onto the street, smiling at Isaac who waited by the lift for her. The hill they lived on had an unusual elevator that ran inside the hill - one of only two earthbound elevators in the world. It was linked to a tunnel, 205 metres long that came out next to the river.

A tower was built next to the elevator. As they walked home, she admired the gold and red of the sky reflected in the river mouth below the tower.

Now she'd finally settled down she could see the beauty of the town. On rare days where the air was particularly still and clear, the mountains of the South Island could be seen from the hill, along with Mount Taranaki to the west and majestic Mount Ruapehu to the north. Joanna felt like she was standing on top of the world.

Married life had begun smoothly with Isaac moving into her house. The days passed by, and they were all happy.

Joanna was the main breadwinner, while Isaac worked part time. Isaac had started a business and had big dreams for it. She was not all that impressed with his efforts so far.

"Where is your business plan, your mentor, and your customers?" she asked him pointedly. She suspected he would not be happy or fulfilled as a provider if it stayed that way, now that he had a family. For now, it worked.

On her last journey through the Kingdom before her marriage, Joanna looked around her. She had come through the desert and the land looked different.

From the high vantage-point the King had led her to, new horizons opened up. The desert gave way to an unknown land that lay behind the hills in front of her. The road did not continue straight on. She saw it end at a kind of 'T' junction.

Joanna did not know where the road would take her, but she was now happy in the town she lived. Her land was now at peace, its borders no longer surrounded by hostile enemies or uncertain friends. There were other people and lands as well, all forming a patchwork within the Kingdom.

She'd changed jobs and was now working at the college campus where she'd studied with Silver-tongue a decade ago, providing first and second level technical support to the students and staff.

Joanna learned from her new boss Mac that Silver-tongue was not liked as a student. He always wanted top marks. Mac said he had been protected by his professional relationship as the tutor from Silver-Tongue's manipulations.

It was a delight to be back there, this time as a member of the staff. The people were great to work with, especially Mac, her former tutor. Joanna thrived under his leadership and words as her morale and self-esteem grew.

The fear of being knifed in the back with words left her and she laughed often. In the Kingdom, she called the campus "Engedi."

It was a year of change. Joanna's sister and brother-in-law Christen and Paul entered Christian Ministry at a Church in Waipawa, not long after Joanna and Isaac's wedding in 2004. It was significant as they knew their roots were in this area.

Joanna and Isaac travelled to Waipawa to witness the ceremony. Standing next to Isaac, she threaded her fingers through his as the thanksgiving prayer began, "Our Father in heaven, we thank you for those who have given us our heritage ..."

Suddenly Joanna found herself transported into the past, even though she was present with Isaac. She saw a woman praying on the hill where they were born. There were immigration barracks behind her and a German sailing ship at anchor at the base of the hill.

"Why am I seeing this?" she asked the Lord, looking at the woman.

"Today you are seeing a generational promise fulfilled," he said referencing Isaiah 61:4-6. "I promised her descendants who would be called as my priests and named as my ministers. Her descendants have been called to rebuild the ancient ruins and restore the places that have been devastated for generations."

Out of fear it was just her imagination, Joanna said nothing about it to Christen or Paul, although she was glad of what she'd seen.

The King had his own plans for Joanna and Isaac.

One weekend Isaac went away to an Alumni weekend at a College north of Auckland he'd attended four years earlier. Joanna did not accompany him because she had to work.

While there, Isaac asked the King for his direction and the next steps to take. The King answered Isaac within a day, telling him he wanted them both to go to college. Scholarships for the first year of a Diploma of Business awaited them.

Isaac said "Thank you Lord, but you had better handle this; she will not take it from me …"

"You WHAT?" Joanna exclaimed when Isaac returned home, telling her about the scholarships.

"I don't want to go to college as a student! It is not on my to-do list. Why can't you do this at the college where I work? We've already studied there, and it's a good place. I knew I should not have let you go up there on your own," she muttered.

"Well, you asked me about my business plan and mentor. That would be the next step …" Isaac replied.

She did not want to leave her job, and did not want to hear about it.

That night, the King spoke to her through his word in Deuteronomy 1:6-8; *"The Lord our God said to us at Horeb; 'You have stayed long enough at this mountain. Break camp."*

"Why do you want me to break camp? I am settled now," she replied.

"See, I have given you possession of the land that I swore I would give to your fathers," he answered.

Joanna tried to ignore him. "Yes, it's great that Christen and Paul have entered ministry in Waipawa; and we can serve you *here*."

The next night the King was waiting for her again, and he was even more specific, speaking from Deuteronomy 2:2; *"You have made your way around this hill country long enough; **now turn north.**"*

"Why do you want me to move now?" Joanna asked; "It's no longer Horeb, a dry and desolate place. It is a place where I've *finally* found happiness."

The Lord replied "I am granting you an open heaven. It is time to go in and take possession of the land."

Although she did not want to uproot herself or the family, she had to consider what the King wanted. She chose to obey after visiting the college and scouting out the land.

The decision to go north came at a great personal cost, but for the first time in her life, it was her decision and not made under compulsion.

She told Mac. Without knowing, he accurately described where she was on the map of the Kingdom. He described Engedi as "a camel stop, an oasis," and said she was right in her decision to take up the scholarship. He went further and acknowledged the Lord saying, "This is the Lord's will."

Her son Justin chose to stay with his father who had recently returned from Australia.

"Why do you not want to come with us?" she asked him, shocked.

"I want to be with Dad," he replied, needing his father.

Joanna understood and hid her sorrow. It felt like her family had split up all over again. Justin stayed with them until the last morning.

"Tell me son; what have you learned in these years with me?" she asked as she drove him to school for the last time.

Justin answered; "I have learned that no matter where I am, I am loved."

She handed her son over to the King and let him go. "Lord, I have raised the boy to know you, to belong to you. No matter what his father says, don't ever let him go. I pray he'll never forget you, or who he is."

The long journey north began on the 4th August 2004, thirty-three years after she left Napier, and ten years to the day of her father's death. She tried not to look back.

Joanna didn't know it then, but the move north was in fulfilment of a promise the Lord had made. He was granting the blessing and promise of an open heaven.

Speaking from Deuteronomy 1:21 (NIV) the King said; *"See, the LORD your God has given you the land. Go up and take possession of it as the LORD, the God of your ancestors, told you. Do not be afraid; do not be discouraged."*

Mahurangi, Open Heaven

Rubbing her bleary eyes, Joanna rolled to her feet and padded to the window. The curtains parted to reveal the grounds of a childcare centre. It was her first glimpse of the campus. They'd arrived in the dark of the early morning hours, after a drive that took nearly twelve hours.

Isaac had rented a horse trailer for their furniture. He knew how to pack the trailer from working for a freight company in Australia. It had been hard deciding what to take, going from a three-bedroom house down to a small student flat. Driving in the dark had been a nightmare.

The weight of the trailer pulled the car's headlights up into the approaching truckers' eyes and they thought their lights weren't dipped. The trailer weighed a ton and the poor old car really struggled on the final hills. It reminded her of her father's efforts moving. They would have fitted in well with his convoy.

Upon arrival they'd fallen on bare unmade beds into an exhausted sleep.

When they awoke to their new lives in the two-bedroom student flat, Isaac asked "Do you want to go to the dining hall for breakfast?"

"No thanks, I'm not up to meeting people just yet. Can you just bring us some food?" she asked.

When she did venture out with her daughter, she found the place had a different vibe from any place she'd ever been. Every person on the campus seemed to know the King. He was spoken of in the lecture theatre, the dining hall, and throughout the campus. It was a Kingdom place.

Warriors casually strode through the place wearing their swords, and there was not a dragon in sight. They all ate together in a big dining hall, and did not have to lock their doors.

The college was small compared to her old college at Engedi, but it punched above its weight, especially in the field of animation. Their credo was "Do it with excellence."

As well as the campus and the childcare centre, there was a church, a farm, a TV station and a home for the intellectually disabled in the nearby town of Warkworth.

The campus was located on a peninsula in the Hauraki Gulf, part of the Auckland isthmus. Kawau Island, a large island with no roads, lay offshore. Auckland lay one hour south by road.

The land was called '*Mahurangi*', which meant 'Open Heaven' in the Maori language. The name suited the land.

Picturesque beaches and bays fringed with Pohutukawa trees dotted the area, and behind the bays there were vineyards, farms, villages and pockets of bush.

The college was constructed by a visionary named Trevor and his wife Jan. In Welsh the name 'Trevor' meant 'great settlement,' which was appropriate.

They were promised work on the campus, but it soon proved to be nothing but a mirage, putting them in a financial bind which she hated.

In the vast desert she'd crossed, mirages meant death. What had she done? Joanna missed her son, her home, the cat, the college at Engedi and her income. It wasn't a good place to start from.

The King sent a woman to her table as she was eating lunch. The woman was visiting her student son and did not know her. "May I bring you a word?" she asked.

Wondering, Joanna nodded.

"You are with him in fellowship with his sufferings. He knows how much you have given up for him. He knows. He is here with you. He is going to bless you."

Grateful for that word, Joanna tried to settle into her new life as an adult student.

Besides the mirage, there were giants in the land. The first giant was an obstacle called statistics; a paper that barred many students from gaining the Diploma of Business.

Looking at what lay before her; she renamed the subject s*adistics*. She sat in the lecture theatre looking at the lecturer blankly – clearly not understanding the paper.

"Do you seriously expect me to learn first year university maths in four weeks - when I have not been able to grasp maths since the age of ten?" Joanna asked the King in disbelief.

"You can do it," he reassured her.

Isaac patiently taught her remedial maths, putting up with the anger, frustration and hurt as painful memories from school tumbled out, haunting her. In her mind, the ghosts from teachers past all agreed she could not learn maths.

The King thought otherwise; "You did not lack ability. Your teachers lacked accountability. They focussed on the children of the parents who expected results," he explained.

Joanna felt cheated. "That sucks," she snarled; "My mother was no match for them, and it ruined my career prospects, until you came along and made me sit that IQ test."

"The teachers did not ruin your career prospects, although they did blight them for a while. You got there in spite of them. Do not believe their words, or allow them to determine your destiny. You have the ability - you always did. Now go make friends with maths," the King encouraged her.

"I can't do it!" Joanna sobbed, beaten back the first time.

"You CAN do it. Get back up and try!" the King urged.

"It's just another programming language!" Isaac told her.

"Well, it's a rubbish language; the rules are not explained and I can't understand the logic," Joanna complained, but Isaac had sown a seed.

"You don't need to understand the logic. You only need the rules," Isaac patiently explained.

Joanna got it. She'd learned several programming languages, quite easily. If she could learn those, she could learn the rules.

"Throw your heart over the bar, and your body will follow," the King said, reminding her of what he'd taught her.

She came back at the giant obstacle and ran hard at it, throwing her heart over the bar. This time, helped by the King and Isaac, she soared over it, hitting a top mark.

"What have you learned?" the King asked afterwards, smiling at the triumphant princess.

"I've learned not to believe negative people who say I can't do something. You strengthen me and say I *can* do it. With you, I can scale a wall!" Joanna replied.

"I have learned that I can do all things through the power of Christ which strengthens me." (Philippians 4:13)

Treasures of darkness

Putting her books away, Joanna plumped down on the sofa.

"I'm glad that's the last paper for the year, but now what do we do? It's the summer holidays, and we have to be off the campus over December and January, with no income. What are we going to do for accommodation?" she asked.

"Let's ask the Lord," Isaac suggested.

"Go camping," the Lord replied, pleased they'd asked him.

Trusting in his leading they spent the last of their money on some camping equipment, leaving the campus before Christmas 2005.

They camped near the Karangahake Gorge, an area of outstanding natural beauty where gold was once mined. It was the place of two rivers. The sparkling Ohinemuri River cut through one gorge while the Waitawheta River tumbled through the other. History was everywhere in the mining ruins and tracks, and there were lots of tunnels to explore.

"We need a torch," Joanna said, groping blindly in the dark of a tunnel and thinking of her poor grandfather. She didn't know that the track through the tunnel dropped about half a metre in front of her.

Just as she was about to step over the edge, she heard a voice behind them; "Stop, there's a drop directly ahead of you." It was a Department of Conservation employee who'd chanced upon them. He edged past with a torch.

"I'm so glad you happened upon us. You saved me from taking a terrific tumble in the dark," Joanna told the guide.

She also thanked the Lord silently behind their unofficial guide's back.

The Lord replied, "*I will lead the blind by ways they have not known, along unfamiliar paths I will guide them; I will turn the darkness into light before them and make the rough places*

smooth. These are the things I will do; I will not forsake them."
Isaiah 42:16 (NIV)

Their guide had a bunch of keys to the locked tunnels. "Would you like to see the mine head?" he asked, leading them into daylight high above the sparkling river.

"Oh, wow! That would be wonderful," they answered, jumping at the opportunity.

"This place has been hidden for over a century," he told them, opening the gate. They peered into the darkness at the mine head and glow worms.

Joanna thanked the Lord again at the campsite.

The King replied from Isaiah 45:3 (NIV); "*I will give you hidden treasures, riches stored in secret places, so that you may know that I am the LORD, the God of Israel, who summons you by name.*"

They left the gorge driving south, meandering their way through the North Island. The Lord led them to many beautiful places, eventually bringing them to Waipawa, a pretty little town in central Hawkes Bay where her sister Christen and brother-in-law Paul had moved the year before.

They were going on holiday and the house was theirs to house sit.

"Look at this," Joanna remarked as she walked around the town with Christen; "Our family name is on the monuments."

"We are known here. When I give them my maiden name, they know of our family," Christen told her.

Having been born and bred in Hawkes Bay, Joanna and Christen knew their forefathers had settled near Waipawa.

"It will be nice to live in an area where we have history," Joanna observed.

"Yes, right from the start I've had a sense of belonging," Christen agreed, glad that their first ministry position was at Waipawa.

"How's it going with the church?" Joanna asked.

"Great, I love being in ministry - although my position is unofficial. Paul is the one who got the job," Christen answered.

"God knows the work you're doing. I know that he's got you here for a reason," Joanna reassured her, thinking of the vision she'd received the year before at their ordination.

Waipawa welcomed them in the summer days that followed. Christen and Paul found Isaac some work on a house renovation. After working on a roof while Joanna took the teenagers swimming, Isaac came home smiling, his face made pink from the sun.

"Why do you look so happy when I'm the one that got to go to the beach?" she laughed.

"I don't know, but I feel I belong here," Isaac answered.

"I feel the same way" Joanna responded.

The next day Joanna explored the Museum with Nicole, her fourteen-year-old daughter. The museum was housed in the old bank.

"I'm glad you like going to museums with me," Joanna said as they wandered around. "Are you feeling the history?" she asked. "I am ..." she paused. Lifting her eyes from her daughter she gazed out the window at the main street of Waipawa.

An old wooden clock ticked slowly on the wall. She looked around the room their ancestor Wilhelm had been in over a century ago.

There was something here ... but not something she could put her finger on.

"What is this place in the Kingdom? Where am I?" she asked the King.

"You'll see. You're near a forgotten gate; a gate that has been closed for over a century ..." he replied.

"Can you guide us to the gate?" she asked, intrigued.

Exploring the land the next day, they came to an out of the way place called Makaretu. For years the surrounding land had called out to her, but now it started to 'sing'.

Joanna had never been to Makaretu, but she remembered the name as the place her forefathers had settled after leaving Germany. The forest had long since gone. Nothing was there, just fields and the odd farmhouse. In the distance the Ruahine Mountain range, her father's birthplace, provided a blue backdrop to the scene.

Traveling the empty road, Joanna spied a cemetery and a memorial gate. The call of the land grew insistent. "Stop the car!" she urged Isaac.

Walking through the gate, Isaac watched Joanna walk around the cemetery as if she was being led. Stopping at a nameless headstone she started scraping.

He wandered around while she scraped at the lichen, her heart thumping as the family name slowly appeared. "It's my name!" she exclaimed, knowing only one family with her surname had come out from Germany. It had to be her great-great grandparents.

Isaac came to help.

"It's Wilhelm's grave," she said, her eyes shining.

"Anna is buried here too," Isaac said, scraping at the lower half of the headstone with the car key.

"Anna! I wish I could tell you that your vater became my father with your help ..." Joanna whispered, paying her respects, thinking of how far they'd come from their birthplace. The call of the land was replaced by a refrain. A feeling of something important ... something left forgotten and unfinished nagged at her.

She met the King's eyes as he stood on the other side of the grave.

"You led us here for a reason, didn't you?"

The King said, *"They died in faith, not having received the promises, but having seen them afar off were assured of them, embraced them and confessed that they were strangers and pilgrims on the earth.*

For those who say such things declare plainly that they seek a homeland.

And truly if they had called to mind that country from which they had come out, they would have had opportunity to return.

But now they desire a better, that is, a heavenly country. Therefore, I am not ashamed to be called their God, for I have prepared a city for them." (Hebrews 11)

The King added, *"Now hear this, I will grant my blessing. I will not deal with your people as I did in the past.*

Just as you have been an object of cursing among the nations, so will I save you, and you will become a blessing. Now do not be afraid, but let your hands be strong." (Zechariah 8:13)

Joanna looked at the King with a question in her eyes.

Did he mean by cursing that although their name was on the war monuments in the area, there was the stigma of being German during the world wars? Or did he mean something far worse, like Freemasonry?

Freemasonry offered a man brotherhood, light, and secrets - but when a man swore allegiance at the lodge, he swore allegiance to a different god. It brought cursing; oaths that bound a family for generations.

The darkness spread throughout the land, for with every New Zealand town, a lodge competed with the church. In recent years she'd discovered that her grandfather and great grandfather had belonged to a lodge. She'd broken off the oaths they made after losing two female cousins to strange cancers, both of who had died at the age of 41.

Joanna regarded the King and spoke; "It does seem we were cursed. Other settler families have farms they've been on for generations.

We don't have land here to call our own, and even though our name is on the war monuments in this area, there's no one left in our line to carry the name. I read the curses you wrote for following other gods; cancer, madness, blindness and confusion. We've had it all. I've seen my people die years before their time. At midday my blind Grandfather groped in the dark, my poor brother was driven mad; and I've been oppressed and robbed.

"Lord you have brought over us a deep sleep: You have sealed your eyes, you have covered our ears," she said, praying the word of Isaiah 29:11.

Will you awaken us and restore the vision?" she asked.

"I will," the King replied; "As for the oaths you removed, you've not come far enough ... I want you to come forward for my blessing."

His voice was rough with emotion, as he extended his hand to her across the grave, speaking from Psalm 103:13-18.

As a father has compassion on his children, so I the LORD have compassion on those who fear me; for I know how you are formed, I remember that you are dust.

The life of mortals is like grass, they flourish like a flower of the field; the wind blows over it and it is gone, and its place remembers it no more.

But from everlasting to everlasting my love is with those who fear me; and my righteousness with their children's children— with those who keep my covenant and remember to obey my precepts.

"I promised to establish your family and love them like a father. I keep my promises, looking to each generation to fulfill my word; and I call until my voice gets hoarse."

Joanna nodded in understanding. She'd already begun to experience the Father's blessing. How could she fulfill his word?

Her mind went back to the tunnel, the guide and the locked gate, "I don't know what you promised. But I do know you are a faithful God, and your promises are for all generations. Please give the blessing you promised."

A monarch butterfly alighted just then on a bush with purple flowers. Choosing some of the flowers, she left them on the grave, saying, *"The grass withers, the flowers fade, but the word of our God stands forever." Isaiah 40:8 9 (NKJ)*

"Would you like me to open the gate?" the Lord asked with a key in his hand, but Joanna had taken her mind off him. A thought came into her mind about a key. "Are you ready to go?" she asked Isaac, looking at the car key in his hand.

The seed

Later in the year 2006, Joanna stood at Isaac's side at graduation with her hard-won Diploma, her eyes seeking out her children.
It would have been perfect if she had been able to beat Isaac, the Dux of the Business course, but the recount mark on the Statistics exam wasn't included in the aggregate scores.
"I would have beaten you if not for Statistics," she teased him.

After completing the Diploma of Business and leaving the campus at the onset of winter, they found a place to rent - a little white cottage on the main road. It would be a good location for the business – if they could afford to get it started.

Their money had been depleted by the mirage and two years of living on a student allowance. They did not yet have jobs. Some of the furniture did not survive the move and had to be replaced. They needed a sofa, washing machine, fridge, and lawnmower.

Joanna looked at their depleted bank account after forking out for the bond, rent in advance, plus a week's rent to the property agent for their 'services'.

There was precious little left. The minimal earnings from their student allowances plus the small amount earned from her part time job did not allow them to recover the costs of going to college.

She was worried as she stated the obvious; "There is no money to start the business. How are we going to build the business and earn money in the meantime?"

Isaac's request to the King was short and sharp; "God, we need some money!"

The next day, Isaac's bank rang. The bank had some money for Isaac from a mortgage insurance policy that had been overpaid years ago. Joanna was amazed. It was enough to keep them going for the rest of the month. A refund from the College for overpaid accommodation kept them going for another month.

The King provided for them until they could get jobs at night.

Despite the financial miracles she still had the jitters. The mirage had taken its toll.

It took a lot for her to come back from that place and learn to trust the King to provide. "God helps those who help themselves!" she'd been told growing up.

The King said; *"So do not worry, saying, 'What shall we eat?' or 'What shall we drink?' or 'What shall we wear?' For the pagans run after all these things, and your heavenly Father knows that you need them. But seek first his kingdom and his righteousness, and all these things will be given to you as well."* Matthew 6:31-33 (NIV)

Not long after that they received a bill from the accountant for his services. How could it be that much when they did not even have a business?

Furious with Isaac who had prematurely hired him before he left City College; she threw the bill that was now up to $1550 onto the floor, slammed the door in his face and walked along the street.

The King caught up with her at the beach. He understood her frustration and anger.

"How are we going to start this company when the accountant is taking all of our hard-earned seed money?" she snapped, exasperated and disillusioned. "You know we need that money to start our business!" she added, kicking the sand.

"I AM going to provide!" the King replied, unable to reassure her, or get through the fog of her black mood.

She sacked the accountant after that, telling Isaac, "We can't afford him. What did we go to college for? I have learned enough to do the books myself, and I can do the tax returns. We'll have to do it ourselves, until the business is established."

Not long after that, the College founders called them to a meeting at the lecture theater with great eagerness and excitement. Jan's eyes shone, as they described the fund that was going to be available for the business students.

The seed capital bore the symbol of the acorn - and it was named in memory of their son who like her brother, had died young. Joanna looked at the acorn, remembering the seed the King had revealed ten years ago after she'd bought her house.
"You will know what it is and when to plant it," he'd told her.
It was to replant the waste fields.

"So, this is why you had us go to College!" she said, her eyes shining like Jan's.

"Was this your plan all along - that I should be self employed as a business owner along with Isaac?" she asked.

In the families she'd been in, the men ran the businesses without their wives.

"I wrote in my book that women own property and run businesses. They are respected figures in their own right, not shadows of their husbands," the King answered, quoting from Proverbs 31 (NIV);

"The noble wife considers a field and buys it; and out of her earnings she plants a vineyard. She sees that her trading is profitable, and her lamp does not go out at night."
Joanna thought about her first husband's business in Sydney. There had been no place for her in the family business except as an unpaid factory labourer on weekends. She did not have any say in how it was run.

She'd been forced to give up everything for their business, and had come away with nothing to show for all the sacrifice. Feeling the pain and regret of her past, she quoted the Song of Solomon 1:6 (NKJ); *"They made me the keeper of the vineyards; but my own vineyard I have not kept."*

Resting his hand on her shoulder, the King said "I promised you a vineyard from out of the wilderness, when I said that I would make the Valley of Achor a door of hope." (Hosea 2:14-16) He rested his other hand on Isaac's shoulder; "I brought you together as a team. You are the partner I spoke of before he met you the second time around.

He has confidence in you, as do I;
'Her husband has full confidence in her and lacks nothing of value. She brings him good, not harm, all the days of her life. Her husband is respected at the city gate, where he takes his seat among the elders of the land.'"
Proverbs 31:11-12 (NIV)

The Year of Inheritance

Tossing and turning, Joanna wished she was at home in her own bed. It was their first year of being in business, and they had to work nights to support themselves - stacking supermarket shelves and cleaning commercial premises. Joanna also had a weekend job as a caregiver for five intellectually disabled people. The work involved a sleepover, which was where she was now.

Sleep eluded her as she tried to quiet her mind. Still awake an hour later, she sighed and crept into the Kingdom looking for the King. "Lord, I need to speak to you about inheritance."

The church had declared 2007 as the year of inheritance - with promises fulfilled, victories obtained, answers received, influence granted, mantles taken up and vision birthed. They talked about it every Sunday.

"I know you spoke of this at Wilhelm and Anna's grave. But why are you getting the church to preach on it for a whole year? What am I missing?" Joanna asked.

Walking into the Kingdom in a dream, Joanna found herself in a place she'd never been before - a misty field lit up by a light. It appeared to be pre-dawn.

The arc of light revealed a race track, where she could hear the sound of an unseen crowd in the grandstands.

A woman came into the light holding a baton, imploring Joanna to believe and reach out. Hesitating, knowing it was Anna, Joanna awaited the King's instructions.

The dragon sneered, saying, "You have a *big* imagination. It is written that the dead know not anything." He was absolutely right.

Looking askance at the King, Joanna backed away, asking him to confirm what she'd seen.

The King's answer came later that morning at church. Rachel, one of the Pastors, had a message to preach. Joanna noticed a plunger in her hands. "This is really the end of our drain plunger, but for the purposes of this morning, this is a relay baton!" Rachel declared, waving it around with a cheeky grin. "I am going to talk about inheritance in terms of receiving the baton and running the race...."

"Are you serious?" Joanna asked, dumbfounded; her eyes fixed on the drain plunger.

The Lord didn't have to answer.

Joanna's heart thudded as she listened intently.

Rachel spoke of those that had gone before - the settler women, and the price they'd paid to come to this country; "These women left their homes, left the comfort of all they knew, of an established and civil society, to go with their husbands into the New Zealand bush.

They lived in extreme hardship, poverty and isolation. I could see their faces, and I could see a baton in their hands."

Anna came into view, holding the baton. This time Joanna allowed herself to believe.

Rachel taught from Hebrews 11 about the race, and about faith; "This is our day, this is our hour. If we just say we're going to remember what a great work they did and make a monument to them, we're not fulfilling biblical inheritance - because we should be advancing the Kingdom of God unlike any day that's even been seen by this nation.

Look at the team we are running with; 'they through faith conquered kingdoms, administered justice, and gained what was promised; who shut the mouths of lions, quenched the fury of the flames, and escaped the edge of the sword; whose weakness was turned to strength; and who became powerful in battle and routed foreign armies.'

They didn't receive what was promised. *'These were all commended for their faith, yet none of them received what had*

been promised. God had planned something better for them so that only together with us would they be made perfect.'"
(Hebrews 11:33, 35, and Hebrews 11:39)

"Do you know what this means?" she asked, "Whether they receive their prize is dependent on us. They're dependent on us! The individual runners do not win the prize for their leg of the race; it is dependent on the last runner - and only *then* does the whole team receive the prize. No pressure," she laughed; "and *they* are watching *us* in the grandstands of heaven."

"This is a different leg of the relay," she continued, "We are born for such a time as this. We need the Isaachar anointing, to understand the days we are living in. The sons of Isaachar discerned the times and knew what to do.

We are part of the generation who will run the last leg of the race. The best runner is saved for the last leg, and the enemy knows this. He also has saved his best for the last leg, and there will be an increase of wickedness.

The dark is getting darker. The King has saved his best wine for last. This is symbolic of our generation.

We need to train; *'Do you not know that in a race all the runners run, but only one gets the prize? Run in such a way as to get the prize. Everyone who competes in the games goes into strict training. They do it to get a crown that will not last, but we do it to get a crown that will last forever.*

Therefore, I do not run like someone running aimlessly; I do not fight like a boxer beating the air. No, I strike a blow to my body and make it my slave so that after I have preached to others, I myself will not be disqualified for the prize.'" 1 Corinthians 9:24-27 (NIV)

"Watch out for that pukey prosperity gospel," Rachel warned, "It could get us off track. We could even end up running on the wrong team.

This preoccupation of self is not producing the spiritual muscle. We have to harden up, learn to say no, learn to resist.

The dominant message of 'prosper, accumulate wealth, get all the toys you want, love life, have fun', has been overemphasised to the detriment of the Church.

It sells a lot of books, and pulls big crowds, but it is to the detriment of our spirit. That would not have washed with the generations that had gone before."

'Therefore, since we are surrounded by such a great cloud of witnesses, let us throw off everything that hinders and the sin that so easily entangles. And let us run with perseverance the race marked out for us.' Hebrews 12:1

After that Joanna entered the Kingdom. The Lord took her to a hidden place which had been locked for over a century. Taking the proffered key from him, she opened the gate and stepped onto the track. Anna should not have come into Joanna's field of vision like this, but here she was, and she'd had her answer at church.

Nodding to Anna, Joanna knelt before the King. "I will run this part of the race, I will run for those who can't," she replied, thinking of her brother.

As she took the baton, a Monarch butterfly flew through an open heaven, to complete the journey its ancestor had begun. It soared upwards, finding the wind.

Joanna looked up, knowing that one day the big questions would be answered.

The King said; *"What you see now is like a dim image in a mirror; then you shall see face-to-face. What you know now is only partial; then it will be complete—as complete as God's knowledge of you." 1 Corinthians 13:12 (GNT)*

"Why did you pick me to run?" she asked.

The King replied, *"You took me at my word - and I choose the foolish things of the world to shame the wise; I choose the weak things of the world to shame the strong," (1 Corinthians 1:27).*

Joanna nodded. "Well, I qualify then. Why did you give me a drain plunger?" she asked with a wry smile.

"If you'd asked me at Waipawa to open the locked gate, you would have received the baton a bit earlier," he replied smiling.

"Yes, I missed the clue, and now I have a drain plunger. Well, at least I can see you've got a sense of humour. I have it on faith that this *is* a baton. I hope I'm not running this leg of the race with a drain plunger!" she remarked, smiling.

He smiled back saying; "It will be whatever I give you."

Joanna looked to see what he'd given her, expecting to see the shepherd's staff. She was surprised to see she carried a pen.

"How can I advance the Kingdom of God?" she asked.

"Tell your sister about the vision, and then write it for others…"

'And the LORD answered me, and said, write the vision, and make it plain upon tablets, so he may run that reads it.'" Habakkuk 2:2 (NKJ)

"I have something else for you," he added, placing a pair of shoes before Joanna and fitting them to her feet. They were made of light but tough material, with a good tread for the mountains.

"Are these for running?" Joanna asked.

"They are the shoes of the good news of peace, for publishing, to help bring the message of the Kingdom," he answered;

How beautiful upon the mountains are the feet of him that brings good tidings, that publishes peace; that brings good tidings of good, that publishes salvation; that says unto Zion, Your God reigns!" NKJ2000

He added; "*The Good News about the Kingdom will be preached throughout the whole world, so that all nations will hear it; and then the end will come …*" *(Matthew 24:14)*

"And you will return," Joanna marvelled, looking at the King in awe.

Beyond handsome, he had black hair and his appearance was of brilliant radiant beauty. Anointed with the oil of joy, his robes were fragrant with myrrh and aloes and cassia.

She said, "*You are the most excellent of men and your lips have been anointed with grace, since God has blessed you forever. Gird your sword on your side, you mighty one; clothe yourself with splendour and majesty.*

In your majesty ride forth victoriously in the cause of truth, humility and justice; let your right hand achieve awesome deeds. Let your sharp arrows pierce the hearts of the king's enemies; let the nations fall beneath your feet.

Your throne, O God, will last forever and ever; a sceptre of justice will be the sceptre of your kingdom." *(Psalm 45, NIV)*

"Is there anything you want to add?" she asked.

"Yes," the King answered, "*I live in a high and holy place, but also with the one who is contrite and lowly in spirit, to revive the spirit of the lowly and to revive the heart of the contrite.*

I will not accuse forever, nor will I always be angry; for then they would faint away because of me-- the very people I have created.

My thoughts are not your thoughts, neither are your ways my ways. As the heavens are higher than the earth; so are my ways higher than your ways and my thoughts than your thoughts.

Seek me while I can be found, call on me while I am near. Turn to me and be saved, all you ends of the earth; for I am God, and there is no other.

By myself I have sworn, my mouth has uttered in all integrity a word that will not be revoked: Before me every knee will bow; by me every tongue will confess that I am the Lord. They will say of me, 'In the LORD alone is deliverance and strength.' *(Isaiah 45:22-24, NIV)*

Behold, I am coming soon! My reward is with me, and I will give to each person according to what they have done. (Isaiah 55:8 and 57:15, NIV)

I am the Alpha and the Omega, the First and the Last, the Beginning and the End." (Revelation 22)

Joanna bowed again; *'Now to you the King eternal, immortal, invisible, the only God, be honour and glory forever and ever. Amen."*

The End

Epilogue

"It's time to bring you home," Joanna said to Isaac, who hadn't seen his American family since he was a boy. In 2008 they flew to Florida to meet his grandmother. The business had grown well enough to pay for the airfares and they asked the King if he could provide for the rest.

He did more than they asked for or expected. A friend named Grace gifted them an accommodation package she had for Florida and Las Vegas. "The King asked me to gift this to you," she said. There were even tickets for Disneyland.

They left for the States in the winter, as storms lashed the country. Flying on the wings of the dawn, they spent a night crossing the Pacific Ocean. Crossing the international date-line sent them back a day, and then they spent another night flying across the American continent.

On arrival, it took some time to get their bearings and orientation. Jim, the friend from the internet whose computer she'd fixed long distance, came to welcome and help them. His was a friendly and familiar face in a vast and strange land.

When they got to Isaac's grandmother's place, they met a family who knew the King well, and loved him. Joanna saw the joy and tears on Eleanor Isaacson's face as she came forward to embrace her grandson. Isaac was home. She had not seen him since he was a twelve-year-old boy.

I have a new granddaughter," she said in her soft American accent, turning to Joanna and hugging her - making her just as welcome as Isaac's mother Ronaele had. Together, they looked at their ring, which had belonged to Eleanor.

The precious diamond had come full circle.

Shepherds Call

Seven years passed. Healed from the hurt of the past, Joanna went from strength to strength. But she still had bad memories from her childhood.
One day her mother grew seriously ill.
Joanna approached the Lord, concerned about her mother's salvation.
"Father, it's up to you whether she'll pull through this time. I forgive my mother for all the abuse. She wasn't able to be a mother because she was abandoned at the age of three.
Is her name written in your book, the book of life?
She believes in you - but she doesn't *know* you. I want to be able to bring her to you, but I can't reach her. I can hardly go through the four spiritual laws, or walk her down the Roman road. Lord, how can I get her to trust you? You promised that if we lack wisdom, we should ask. I'm asking."

"I will come to her," he replied, pointing to a painting that her mother used to have; a vintage 1900's painting called 'Shepherd's call', which depicted a collie barking for the shepherd after finding a lost lamb in the snow.

"Talk about that painting. Ask her who the dog is barking for, and then bring me in. I want her to know she is the lamb ..."

"What a brilliant idea. I'd never have thought of that," Joanna replied, impressed. "But I don't want religion getting in the way. What should I do if it does?"
"Tell her that true religion is to take care of widows and orphans."
Later Joanna sat at her mother's side, alone.
"You know that painting of the dog and the lamb you had?" she began.
"Yes, I gave it away," her mother replied.
"Yes, you did. Remember that lost lamb?"
"The lamb didn't have a mother," her mother recalled.
"Yes, that's right Mum, she didn't have a mother," Joanna replied, sad for them both at the word 'mother.'
"The Lord said for me to tell you that you are that lamb," she

said, as soon as she'd gathered her composure.
Tears came to her mother's eyes.
"Who was the dog barking for?" Joanna asked.
"The shepherd," her mother eventually answered.
"Did you know the Lord is the Shepherd?" Joanna asked.
More tears came.
Joanna added "Mum, he looks for lost lambs and he saves them. You are that lamb. He wants to lift you up and carry you in his arms, close to his heart."
Just as Joanna had foreseen, her mother talked about religion.
"Mum, do you know what the Bible says true religion is?" Joanna responded.
Her mother shook her head.
"True religion is to take care of widows and orphans," Joanna replied, giving the answer the Lord had given her.
"I'm a widow," her mother said.
"Yes, you are a widow," Joanna replied, impressed at the Lord's answer.
"Who is the Lord to you?" Joanna asked cautiously.
Her mother was silent.
"Are you afraid of death?" Joanna asked.
"Yes, I'm afraid of the devil – I don't want to see him," she replied.
Bringing her back to the Shepherd, Joanna said "Mum, if you accept Jesus as your saviour, you need fear no evil in the Valley of the Shadow of Death.
The Lord will be your Shepherd, and his rod and staff will comfort you."
"Who would *you* like him to be?" she asked, watching her mother's face and remembering her own staff.
"My protector," her mother replied.
"Like a saviour?" Joanna asked.
"Yes," her mother agreed.
"Do you accept him as your saviour?" Joanna asked.
"Yes," her mother replied, with childlike faith.
Outside, a piece of a rainbow shone out from clouds above the Ruahine Mountain range. That night, her mother sang.

An invitation

In ancient times, when one came to seek the king's help or counsel, the servant's job was to open the door to the king's house and assist him in reaching the King. The King's servants have a similar responsibility to assist those who God is calling in coming to the King, Jesus Christ. Let me tell you a story about how important this is;

After leaving Sydney Joanna was led to her distant cousin Leonie, Anna's grand-daughter. They became friends. Leonie's father Albert and Joanna's great-grandfather Walter were brothers. Albert had been turned off the Lord as a young boy when he'd been exposed to religion.

He was the boy in chapter one who'd bitten Ferdi on the thigh while being spanked, causing Anna to leave Ferdi and return to New Zealand with her children.

His mother may have been unable to lead her youngest son Albert to the Lord because of his bad experience with religion, her deafness and the language barrier.

Consequently, Albert's daughter Leonie grew up not knowing the King.
In 1992 Leonie was dying of cancer at the age of 41. There was no servant on hand to guide Leonie to the King - because Joanna didn't want to preach to her. She was not serving the Lord and did not feel she had any authority to represent him.

Joanna found out after her death that Leonie had looked in the Bible for the Lord, but on her own she was unable to find the passage that led to the door.

When she was dying all Joanna was able to say was "Leonie, call out to the Lord. God will not turn you away."

But how could she call on the one they'd not believed in? And how could she believe in the one of whom she had not heard? And how could she hear without someone preaching to her? As it is written: "How beautiful are the feet of those who bring good news!" (Romans 10:14)

How sad the King was to see Leonie search for him in the dark. It's in his heart to have servants available for those who seek him. In memory of Leonie, here is the passage to the door;

If you declare with your mouth, "Jesus is Lord," and believe in your heart that God raised him from the dead, you will be saved. For it is with your heart that you believe and are justified, and it is with your mouth that you profess your faith and are saved. Romans 10:9 NIV

If you are still with me, thank you for reading the book. If you don't know the King, I invite you to follow this passage, and seek the King for yourself. The passage is part of "the Roman Road" from the book of Romans in the Bible.

This is the Roman road;
Romans 3:23, For all have sinned, and fall short of the glory of God.
Romans 6:23, For the wages of sin is death; but the gift of God is eternal life through Christ Jesus our Lord.
Romans 5:8 But God demonstrates his own love for us in this: While we were still sinners, Christ died for us.
Romans 10:9, If you declare with your mouth, "Jesus is Lord," and believe in your heart that God raised him from the dead, you will be saved.
Acknowledge, Believe and Confess.

If you think you are a lost cause, you're not. Look where Joanna was when the King came to help her. We are all sinners who need salvation. The King has come to seek and save the lost. He is here for all who call on his name.

God bless,
Jo Rolston

Glossary

NZ Words
Bogan means lower class
Dock means to remove lambs' tails

Maori words
Whare means house.
Rangi means sky or Heaven.
Taonga means gift.
Tomo means cave.
Mana means honour, respect, authority.
Wharerangi means house of heaven.
Mahurangi means open heaven.

The Author

A computer technician, Joanne ran an IT business with her husband Bert for 15 years, until like many small businesses it ended in 2021 with the final 100-day Covid lockdown of Auckland, NZ.

Her professional interests were in Information Technology and Small Business. She has a Diploma of Business as well as IT qualifications gained in NZ, Australia and the U.S.

Now semi-retired she wants to write more books.

She is a mother of two grown children and has returned to Wanganui, NZ where she lives with her husband Bert and one spoiled cat.

Joanne holds to the Apostles creed in her beliefs.

Her spiritual gifts are writing, discernment and faith.

She likes travel, walking, writing, day tramps in National parks, and playing games of 500.

Her blog is kingdom777.wordpress.com

www.ingramcontent.com/pod-product-compliance
Lightning Source LLC
Chambersburg PA
CBHW060113170426
43198CB00010B/870